THE GREAT
PHILOSOPHERS

THE GREAT
PHILOSOPHERS

JEREMY STANGROOM
JAMES GARVEY

EAGLE EDITIONS

This edition printed in 2006

Published by Eagle Editions Limited
11 Heathfield
Royston
Hertfordshire SG8 5BW

Copyright © 2005 Arcturus Publishing Limited
26/27 Bickels Yard, 151–153 Bermondsey Street, London SE1 3HA

ISBN-13: 978-1-84193-299-6
ISBN-10: 1-84193-299-X

Printed in China

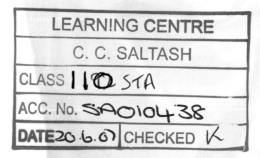

Contents

Introduction

No one is entirely sure what philosophy is. If that's not a reassuring first sentence in a book on thirty-seven great philosophers, it's at least an honest one. There are three sorts of view of what philosophy is, and no broad agreement about which one is right. It's worth wondering about these three answers a little.

Some maintain that philosophy is best defined by its abstract subject matter. Philosophy as traditionally conceived deals with the Big Three Questions. What exists? How do we know? What are we going to do about it? The answers involve us in metaphysics, the study of the nature of reality; epistemology, the study of the conditions required to know something; and ethics, an attempt to say what it is to live a morally good life. These are distinctly human questions in the sense that it is hard to be human without wondering about them at some time or other. Great minds sometimes settle on them, think about them, and the result is philosophy.

Some argue instead that one might philosophize about anything, that philosophy is best defined by a particular method. The method has a lot to do with careful and systematic thinking, giving reasons for conclusions, and getting those conclusions into clear view. Anyone can have a view about what's right or wrong, but the view becomes philosophy if it is explicitly characterized, has some support in reason.

Finally, some take it that philosophy consists in a kind of attitude or way of life. Distinctive of this way of living is a critical view of things, a refusal to accept what others accept without further reflection. It has got more than one great philosopher into serious trouble. Our exemplar here is Socrates, who thought that the unexamined life was not worth living. He not only thought this, he died for it. Many join him in thinking that the word 'philosophy', literally 'love of wisdom', marks out an approach to life as against a method or set of questions.

Someone who plumps for any of these answers will be happy to find representatives of his or her view in this book. Certainly answers to all three Big Questions get a lot of attention, as does the distinctive method of philosophy, as do the lives of philosophers. There is tension here, too, and it's impossible to resolve it. Fans of method will be annoyed to find Nietzsche and Hegel on the list. Proponents of the subject-matter view might blanch at the inclusion of Machiavelli. Those who see philosophy as a way of life will wonder about Bacon and Heidegger.

Nevertheless, the list hangs together. If it's hard to say just what philosophy is, it's easy to spot when you see it. Wittgenstein argues that some terms pick things out not in virtue of a strict definition, but by something like family resemblance. Maybe not everyone in the family album sports a version of grandfather's admirable nose, but it's clear that all are members of the same family. So too with the great philosophers. Philosophy has been under way for more than two thousand years, and in such a long stretch, it would be something of a miracle if all philosophers fitted a single mould.

This book traces the biggest thoughts in the largest and most influential parts of philosophy's long walk through history. You will find here thinkers of the first philosophical thoughts in the West, the Ancient Greek and Early Roman philosophers to whom so much is owed. You will see the way in which their concerns became the concerns of those who followed; the way their answers shaped what we now recognize as philosophy. Mediaeval philosophy makes an appearance, carrying ancient concerns on to Renaissance philosophers, adding an emphasis on religion to the mix. The thinking of the modern era, the modern explosion of philosophy ushered in by Descartes, is well represented here too. Founders and representatives of the rationalist and empiricist schools get a fair hearing, as do the dark conclusions of those who favour scepticism.

The long walk is, thankfully, carrying on, and you will find here the thoughts which make contemporary philosophy what it is, and perhaps what it is on the way to becoming. Philosophy, whatever it is, is certainly still under way, and this book takes account of both the discipline as it is practised now and the history which made contemporary philosophy possible.

Usually, the introduction to a book like this offers some sort of apology for cutting corners, says that it's impossible to characterize fully the thoughts of so many great philosophers in a single place. You also find apologies of another sort, excuses for including some philosophers and not others. You will find no apologies for such obvious and unavoidable facts here. Does it make any sense at all to apologize for a fact or set of facts? This book is written for intelligent people who know what they're getting into when they buy a book. If this book is not the last word on the great philosophers – and what book possibly could be – it is certainly a collection of useful first words. Included with each entry is a list of works you can read if you want to take your study of philosophy further. You won't find any last words there either.

No matter how you view philosophy, regardless of what you think it is, you have here accounts of the lives and thoughts of the very best thinkers in the philosophical neighbourhood, dealing carefully and rationally with the most human of questions, the hardest questions, the questions which matter most.

Socrates

It would be difficult to overestimate the influence of Socrates (470–399BC) on Western philosophy. We know that Socrates was the mentor of the young Plato, and we also know that Plato's writings had deep and lasting effects on virtually the whole of Western thinking.

IRRITATINGLY, IT WOULD ALSO BE DIFFICULT TO OVERESTIMATE our ignorance of Socrates' actual views. Socrates probably wrote next to nothing of a philosophical nature, and, anyway, none of it survives. Our problem, the 'Socratic Problem' as it is called, is that we do not know exactly what Socrates himself believed – it is not clear that he claims to know anything. He even denies being a teacher. So we know he is massively influential, but we do not know the precise nature of that influence. The situation is more than exasperating.

Socrates is believed to have been the son of a midwife and a stone mason. Although he was reduced to poverty in old age, he seems to have enjoyed a reasonably well-off early life. He served as a hoplite (a heavy infantryman) in the Athenian army, so at least at that time in his life he must have owned property and been able to pay for his own equipment. However he made his living, it was not by his looks. He is described variously as pug-nosed, thick-lipped, rotund, his eyes though quick were bulbous, and he seems not to have been devoted to personal grooming. His ability to drink was prodigious and well known.

If what interests us is not his life but his views; there are only three contenders, three reasonable sources of information about Socrates' philosophy, three writers alive in his lifetime. The comic poet Aristophanes is one, but he paints a ridiculous portrait of Socrates, a general caricature and amalgam of philosophers and intellectuals active in Athens at the time. The writings of Xenophon survive, but he characterizes Socrates as nothing more than a vapid repository of homey aphorisms – one wonders how such a man could have troubled the Athenian authorities as much as Socrates in fact did. We have, finally, the dialogues of **Plato**, but even these are problematic. We will follow convention and assume with most commentators (and with a large pinch of salt) that the Socrates of the early dialogues is as near a faithful representation of the views of the actual Socrates as we are likely to have.

However Socrates made his living it was not by his looks; he is described variously as pug-nosed, thick-lipped and rotund.

A New Approach

From those early dialogues, something of the man's views emerges. It is clear that we call those who came before Socrates 'Pre-Socratic' for a reason: his interests differ markedly from the dubious preoccupations of Parmenides, Heraclitus, Anaximander and the like. Rather than speculate on cosmology, affecting dark pronouncements on the nature of the Absolute, Socrates was 'the first to call philosophy down from the heavens', in Cicero's memorable phrase. Socrates worries about this life and how best to live it. His concerns are resolutely practical.

The Early Dialogues

The Socrates of the early dialogues typically strikes up a conversation with one or a few interlocutors which eventuates in a question about the nature of some virtue or other: what is justice, what is piety, what is courage or what is temperance. The interlocutor attempts an answer. Socrates then subjects the answer to critical analysis, usually showing that the answer is inconsistent with something else held by the interlocutor to be true, that it leads to some confusion or other or is plainly lacking in some respect. The Greek word for this pattern of questioning, responding and scrutinizing is 'elenchus', and Socrates was a master of it. According to Xenophon, he 'could do what he liked with any disputant'. Why did he engage in the elenchus? There are a number of answers.

According to one legend, Chaerephon asks the Oracle at Delphi whether anyone is wiser than Socrates, and the surprising answer is that no one is wiser. Socrates, astonished, tries to prove the Oracle wrong by approaching those who profess wisdom and asking them about the virtues. When he reduces each one to confusion, he concludes that the Oracle is right, in a way: Socrates knows he doesn't know anything, whereas others are wrong in thinking they know.

The point of the many encounters, the many arguments, cannot just consist in undermining the self-confidence of prominent Athenians, and indeed we have some hints from the dialogues of Socrates' view of his own activity. Perhaps Socrates really is pursuing definitions. It certainly seems, in places, as though he thinks that only with such definitions in hand can one have the knowledge required to make the right choices in life. Unless we know what justice is, how can we possibly hope to act justly?

We do have the problem of reconciling the fact that Socrates never clearly settles upon a definition, yet he does not consider his efforts failures. The dialogues do not end with a crestfallen Socrates, head in hands, bemoaning his ineptitude. On

MAJOR WORKS

Socrates wrote nothing of a philosophical nature. We can, however, look to Plato's early dialogues – which some take to express Socrates' actual views – for guidance. The following three dialogues together give an account of part of Socrates' philosophy and the way he faced his death. We cannot say just when any were written.

Apology contains Socrates' defence in response to charges of corrupting the youth of Athens and impiety. He also talks

about his beliefs and convictions and the life he has led.

Crito recounts a conversation between Socrates and his friend Crito, which conveys something of Socrates' ethical views.

Phaedo is a very moving account of Socrates' final hours and contains discussions of immortality, the soul, and death.

the contrary, there is often a kind of upbeat satisfaction, even gratitude shown all around to those who have taken the time to reflect with him, something approaching joy and the recognition of time very well spent. Engaging in the co-operative pursuit of definitions is not only of value to him, it is of extraordinary value: the unexamined life, Socrates says as he nears his death, is not worth living. Yet if the aim of the exercise is getting definitions, the examined life is a kind of failure. There is at least one way to resolve this depressing conclusion.

It might well be that a stable definition is not the point and purpose of the exercise at all; perhaps the activity of joint enquiry itself is the aim, examination itself is of value. In other words, it may be that Socrates finds value not in getting at the truth, but looking for it in conversation. One might reasonably wonder why he thinks this. Some maintain that instilling in his companions not truth, but the desire for truth, was the point in the first place. It is worth noting that philosophy as it is conducted now still has a share in this. Lectures at university are accompanied by seminars aimed at discussion. Talks at conferences are followed by questions and answers. Philosophy is still the collective enterprise it was in Socrates' day. Perhaps this is a kind of vindication of this view of his activities.

Socratic Paradoxes

Although no clear and stable definitions materialize, there are some themes, if certainly not doctrines, that emerge in the early dialogues which we might reasonably take to be Socratic. There are many formulations of the co-called 'Socratic paradox' or 'Socratic paradoxes': no one does wrong voluntarily or deliberately; virtue is knowledge; moral weakness is impossible. The line of thought underpinning all versions is this. What is good is beneficial and what is evil or wrong is harmful to us. Doing wrong hurts us, damages what is most valuable in us – our soul. No one really desires what is harmful unless he fails to recognize it as such, unless he mistakes it for something beneficial. All wrong-doing, then, results from ignorance. No one who really knows virtue will act immorally; no one who really understands right and wrong will chose anything other than what is right. Anyone who, in fact, chooses to do something morally wrong does so only in ignorance.

Would this view have been a comfort to Socrates who, at the age of 70, faced his accusers on charges of impiety and corrupting the youth of Athens? It is hard not to wonder. We can do more than wonder about the charges. Socrates professed to have a kind of mystical, divine sign – perhaps something like an inner voice – which warned him against some actions. The Delphic Oracle's pronouncements might have been taken by him as a kind of holy mission. Both of these possibilities might explain a part of the impiety claim.

In what sense did he corrupt the youth? As you might imagine, speculation has abounded. He certainly did gather around him a circle of young men, many the sons of prominent Athenians, quite of few of them staunch antidemocrats. When democratic feeling ran high, it is possible that excuses for the boys' unpopular views were found in the influence of Socrates.

We can also do more than wonder about the motivations of his accusers. Certainly his practice of asking prominent Athenians awkward questions, in broad daylight and in public, about the nature of virtue, reducing them to confusion, suffusing his interrogations with well-known Socratic irony, could not have won him

many influential friends. It is likely that the intention of his accusers consisted in little more than shutting him up. In Plato's record of the trial, it is clear that if only Socrates would agree to stop his philosophizing, he would be free to go, but this is, of course, the one thing he simply cannot do. When given the chance to plead for his life, recommend a punishment for himself other than death, Socrates offers his judges an ethics primer. He suggests that his good works – his interrogations, which have done nothing but improve the moral health of the citizens and therefore the city of Athens – can only be rewarded by putting him up at the expense of the city itself in these his declining years. He seems to have left his judges with no alternative but to condemn him to death. He refuses the opportunity to flee. He drinks the poison and dies.

If we cannot say, exactly, what doctrines Socrates held or how he lived, we know at least from the dialogues that Plato loved him, whoever he was. The portrait he paints is profoundly affectionate. Socrates might have been physically unappealing, but it is hard to imagine a more attractive character: the good humour and conviviality; the devastating skill in debate; the passion for knowledge or at least the will to pursue it anywhere and anytime; patience with those keen to know and little time for fools; the oddness; the integrity which cost him his life.

It is easy to be drawn into the debate, to smile and quietly cheer for Socrates as he brings low some over-stuffed, jet-setting Athenian; to read again difficult parts of his replies in the hope of better understanding him; to put the book down and stare out a bus window, wondering what Socrates would have said had so-and-so replied to his question a little differently. You can easily understand what good company he must have been. Had you been there – sitting in the Athenian sun, listening to the arguments – you would have been corrupted too. No doubt this has much to do with Plato's art, but it is impossible not to suppose, too, that it has something to do with the personality of Socrates.

The Death of Socrates. Socrates comforts his grieving friends by reaffirming his belief in a true and unchanging reality beyond the earthly realm.

It is easy to be drawn into the debate, to cheer for Socrates as he brings low some over-stuffed, jet-setting Athenian.

Plato

It is possible to argue about who is the finest Renaissance painter. It is possible to argue in this way about sculptors, writers, poets, more or less any sort of artist. However, if the question is who writes the best dialogues, then there is no room for controversy. Plato (428–347BC) has no peers.

428–347BC

WHILE IT IS TRUE THAT A HANDFUL OF PHILOSOPHERS HAVE HAD A STAB at writing dialogues, and some such works are of serious philosophical interest, there really is no comparing them to Plato's writings. Plato has the possibly singular distinction of simultaneously inventing and bringing to perfection a kind of art.

It is clear that things might have been different. Plato was probably destined for a career in politics or at least public life. His father, Ariston, was allegedly descended from the last king of Athens. Some sources report that his mother, Perictione, was a relative of the Athenian statesman Solon. When his father died, Plato's mother married a friend of Pericles. Plato had an impressive pedigree, and his family was well connected and wealthy. It is sometimes said that the injustice surrounding the execution of Plato's mentor, Socrates, led Plato to reject public life and pursue philosophy. We know that Plato and some of his relatives and associates were staunch antidemocrats, and following the fall of the 30 Tyrants, antidemocratic sentiments were not rewarded in Athens. So it is also possible that it was the lack of opportunity for people with his political leanings that kept Plato out of political life. We simply do not know.

Early Life

Little is known about much of Plato's life. It is likely that he undertook military service, possibly as a member of the Athenian cavalry in action against Sparta. The image of Plato thundering into battle on horseback is not an easy one to come to grips with, but it is worth remembering that 'Plato' was a nickname, meaning 'broad' or 'wide' – a reference to his broad shoulders. So he might have been something of a warrior. His actual name was Aristolces. But for a nickname that stuck, English might have been lumbered with 'Aristolcic relationships'.

We know that he travelled, probably to Egypt and certainly to Syracuse. Seneca reports that he suffered an illness as a result of his travels late in life, but whether or not this killed him is an open question – it seems unlikely. We also know that he and a few others founded the Academy in 385BC, widely considered the first university but probably nothing of the sort. According to some reports, 'The Academy' was actually the name of Plato's house, and it seems likely that he and only a few like-minded individuals took on a small number of students and offered private tuition. It is not clear that Plato actually lectured there – in his writings, Aristotle, a student at the Academy for 20 years, mentions only the dialogues when considering Plato's views, as opposed to lectures or discussion. At any rate, the place would have been unlike a modern or even medieval university in nearly all respects. Nevertheless, it did have a remarkable lifespan, continuing for nine hundred years. That tireless promoter of Christianity, the Roman Emperor Justinian, considered it a pagan institution and saw to it that its doors were finally and permanently closed.

If little reliable information about his life has come down to us, we are staggeringly fortunate in having probably all the dialogues he wrote. They are usually organized into at least three periods, though the precise ordering is a matter of continuing controversy. **Socrates** is the main figure and hero in most. The so-called 'early' dialogues are thought to reflect the historical Socrates' own interests, but in the middle and later periods Socrates becomes more and more a mouthpiece for Plato. Nevertheless, it is clear that Socrates casts a very long shadow over Plato, and some of Plato's most profound insights are attempts to deal with Socratic worries, or at least worries emerging from Socratic interests.

Although we use the word 'blue', how did we learn to do so, when we never encounter an unambiguous example?

Defining the Virtues

The early dialogues have Socrates searching for definitions of the virtues, motivated by the view that one must know what, for example, justice is before one can hope to act justly. It is worth noting that Socrates never finds an acceptable definition, and it is possible that this raises a difficulty which Plato's middle and later works attempt to answer. Other difficulties, closely connected, probably motivated Plato too. We will have a look at a few of them; for example, our use of a general term like 'blue'.

We apply the word 'blue' to a variety of things, but how on earth did we learn to do so when we never actually encounter an unambiguous example of blue? Everything we see is blue and cold or blue and bitter or blue and small: how then did we learn to use the word 'blue' in the first place?

MAJOR WORKS

We probably have all of Plato's dialogues, but we really cannot say when each one was written. The following are among the most important of Plato's works.

Republic is without doubt Plato's masterpiece. It begins with a consideration of the nature of justice and quickly becomes an extended consideration of politics, epistemology, and much else.

Symposium is not representative of the dialogues, containing as it does a series of speeches at a slightly drunken dinner party, rather than the full-on Socratic debate of most of Plato's other dialogues, but it is among the most beautiful things ever written. It takes as its topic the nature of love.

Meno deals with virtue, knowledge and the relation between them.

Parmenides contains an interesting critique of Plato's Theory of Forms, including the famous Third Man Argument. It is worth reading if only for the opportunity to see Socrates seem to lose an argument.

Theaetetus takes up the topics of knowledge and wisdom. It concludes with some instructive thoughts on the point of Socratic dialectic.

Or consider what we take to be our knowledge of something blue, let us say, for instance, my mundane knowledge that my shirt is blue. It is fairly clear that the world around us is constantly changing. My blue shirt will be washed and washed; it will begin to fade, and soon it won't really be the same fetching blue that it is today. I might inadvertently wash it with something else that is not colour fast, something bright orange, in which case my faded shirt will not even be blue at all. Regrettably, in the fullness of time, it won't even be a shirt anymore, returning, as all things must, to dust. Two questions arise from all this.

First, as my shirt fades, what standard do we use to say, truly, that it is not as blue as it was? As my shirt falls apart and looks less and less like a shirt (perhaps more and more like a rag), what standard do we use to say, truly, that it is not a shirt anymore? Some unchanging standard seems needed to make sense of these judgements, but what could do the job in this changing world?

If something is truly known, it is known forever; it cannot turn out to be false tomorrow.

Second, it seems that a proposition known could never become false. Opinions certainly could change, as do fashions, but if knowledge is possible, the objects of knowledge must themselves be unchanging. If something is known, it is known forever. 'Two plus two equals four,' 'Triangles have three sides,' 'Bachelors are unmarried, adult males': all these propositions are true, and they cannot turn out to be false tomorrow. Knowledge, thought Plato, is above the fluctuating vagaries of this imperfect world. How could this be? What ensures that knowledge is fixed, if everything around us is constantly changing?

The Theory of Forms

Plato's Theory of Forms is an attempt to deal with all of this, and the solution is radical. He claims that real, mind-independent entities exist – forms of things like Justice, Good, Beauty, Triangle, Blue, Bachelor, and so on for any general term you like. Socratic interviews really do aim at truth; there are definitions; there is knowledge; words can be learnt; standards underpin judgement; all because there are timeless, stable, perfect, unchanging, intelligible things: Forms. We can hope for an understanding of justice because, literally, Justice exists.

Although you will not find Justice in this vale of tears, you can find acts, people, events and laws which, in some sense, resemble or share in or participate in the Form Justice – indeed, it is this which makes all such things just. You will never see perfect Justice, only shadowy copies, but you might come to an intellectual grasp of Justice by engaging in Socratic dialectic, which now has objects at which to aim. You cannot really be said to know anything about this imperfect world, but the unchanging Forms make possible genuine knowledge of the Good, the Beautiful, and so on. Perfect standards for judgements exist too: one who grasps the Beautiful, say, will be so much the better judge of the shadowy reflections of Beauty in this world.

The Theory of the Forms gets an awful lot of press, but it is true that it only appears in the middle dialogues, and Plato criticizes the view himself in the later dialogues. The best known objection to the theory, the Third Man Argument, runs as follows. Beautiful things in this world are beautiful just in so far as they participate in or resemble the Form of the Beautiful. The Form of the Beautiful, Plato alleges, is itself beautiful. Does this not require some third Form which the Beautiful itself resembles? Socrates and Milo are both men because they resemble something else, the Form Man. But the Form Man must also be a man (or share in manhood), just as the Beautiful itself is beautiful. Does this not require a third thing, a Third Man, which the Form Man must resemble in order for it, too, to be a man? The regress thus initiated looks viscous and infinite.

The Theory of Forms, whether or not it overcomes this objection, figures in many of Plato's dialogues. Although it might an oversimplification, some argue that the theory provides him with the groundwork for almost everything else he writes about, and the breadth of Plato's philosophical interests is genuinely astonishing. He formulates a general metaphysical outlook, a conception of the soul as immortal (and thus able to visit the realm of Forms), a view of learning as recollection, a complex epistemology, a theory of mathematics, an objectivist ethics, a highly detailed and nuanced (if perhaps disturbing) political philosophy, views on society, a theory of mind, a methodology. Think of any of the usual subdivisions of philosophical enquiry, and Plato has a view on at least a part of it.

Plato's Importance

A.N. Whitehead famously remarked that the safest characterization of Western thought is that 'it consists of a series of footnotes to Plato'. It has been said since that this is an exaggeration, but not an outrageous one. Others find Plato a little wishy-washy, preferring the tough-minded and careful analysis of **Aristotle** to the allegorical excesses of Plato's dialogues. Some grumble a little and say they would rather have the beauty of an argument than the beauty of a metaphor. Whatever one makes of the value of Plato's writings, it is clear that they have travelled well. One still smiles and grimaces, agrees and objects, at all the right places, all the places Plato intended when he wrote the dialogues 2,000 years ago. It is difficult to imagine anyone writing today who will be read in AD4,000. If there is anything like a university around in that distant year, it is sometimes said, we can be certain that Plato will be required reading.

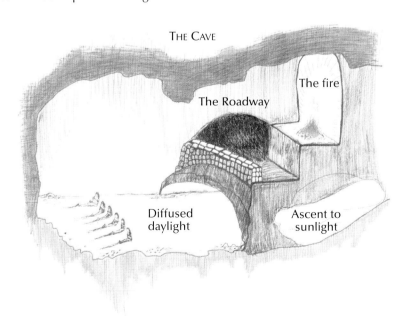

THE CAVE

The fire

The Roadway

Diffused daylight

Ascent to sunlight

The Myth of the Cave: Plato's prisoners sit and watch the shadowplay on the wall of the cave, convinced that what they are seeing is reality.

Aristotle

Imagine that you are Plato, coming to the end of your years, presiding over the now-famous Academy, enjoying a reputation among both your students in particular and Athenians in general. You hear, perhaps while lingering in a doorway, a murmured reference to the 'Reader', the 'Mind of the Academy'.

384–322BC

THEY ARE NOT TALKING ABOUT YOU, BUT A YOUNG UPSTART FROM THE STICKS, perhaps only seventeen years old, called 'Aristotle'. Would you find this galling?

In truth, we can only speculate about the relationship between Plato and Aristotle (384–322BC). We know that Aristotle's father, a physician to the court of the King of Macedon, sent him to Athens when he was about 17 and that he joined the Academy, remaining there for 20 years, first as a student and eventually as a teacher. In the year that Plato died, Aristotle departed – no one knows whether he remained out of loyalty to Plato and left on the master's death, or departed in disgust, having not been offered control of the school. We do know that his father's connections led him to Macedonia, to tutor a 13-year-old, the future Alexander the Great.

After years of travel and study, he returned to Athens and founded the Lyceum or peripatetic school – so named either because lectures were conducted on the move or in honour of the locale's fine walkways. Here he remained until 323BC, when, so the story goes, his Macedonian connections and Athens' anti-Macedonian mood led to his being formally charged with impiety – Athens being nothing if not consistent. Allegedly claiming that he would not let the city sin twice against philosophy, he fled to Chalcis, where he died the following year.

Aristotle not only invented whole disciplines, he invented the very notion of a discipline as such.

He produced an enormous body of work. Ancient commentators distinguish between his esoteric and exoteric writings – the former were highly technical pieces, written for use within the school, and the latter well-crafted pieces for public consumption. We know he wrote dialogues. We have Cicero's word that the public works were things of beauty, a 'golden river of eloquence'. No such work survives. We have only his technical, esoteric writings, and these are not beautiful in the usual sense, but are compact, crammed with jargon and what seem like technical preoccupations, stilted, and generally lacking in literary virtue. Actually, we have what are probably his lecture notes. They are works in progress, edited by those who came after, and discrepancies and inconsistencies sometimes confound us. Few, though, would be willing to trade even a scrap of it for a part of the public writings: though rough-going, Aristotle's surviving writings are crammed with the fruits of an incredible intellectual power.

The Rules of Logic

Aristotle more or less invented and formalized the rules of right reasoning, the beginnings of philosophical logic. He was the first to study the nature of deduction, to say what it means for a proposition to follow of necessity from premises, to identify and formalize different possible sorts of syllogism. With a general notion of proof in hand, he formalized the relation between the evidence gathered by studying things in the world and coming to true conclusions about those things. In doing this, he did much more than point us in the direction of what we now recognize as science. This alone would have been beyond impressive and earned him a large place in history, but his writings on logic and methodology constitute only a part of the Aristotelian corpus. Aristotle was just getting started when he invented science.

He wrote enormously influential treatises on ethics, politics, metaphysics, physics, mathematics, psychology, poetry, rhetoric, aesthetics, meteorology, geology, methodology, cosmology, philosophy of mind, theology, psychology, memory, and dreams, among much else. It is not going too far to say that he invented entire disciplines, whole regions of enquiry which still occupy us. More than this, Aristotle was the first to engage in the practice of distinguishing between different subject-matters; recapitulating and considering a topic's intellectual history; explicitly identifying the standards of evidence, degrees of precision, questions, and so on proper to each. Aristotle not only invented whole disciplines, he invented the very notion of a discipline as such.

All of this is to say nothing of his biological writings, which constitute perhaps a quarter of what we have. In a letter to William Ogle, a famous translator of Aristotle's biological works, Darwin mentions his 'two gods' Linnaeus and Cuvier, concluding that they were 'mere schoolboys to old Aristotle'. It took a lot of thinking, nearly two thousand years of thinking, to get beyond Aristotle's teleological or goal-directed conception of life and the parts of animals. All of it follows from his famous four causes. The word 'cause' is a little misleading, and one might just think of the four causes as the four explanatory features of a thing that we get by asking four sorts of question.

Questions of Nature

To use Aristotle's example, we might ask four questions about a statue: what is it made of (bronze: its material cause); what sort of thing is it (a statue: its formal cause); what brought it into being or initiated the changes that led to its being what it is (a sculptor: its efficient cause); and what is it for (decoration: its final cause). One gets a feeling from this that Aristotle is preoccupied with goals and ends, and it is true that Aristotle denies that we really know a thing, even a natural object or organ, until we know what it is for, what it aims at or does.

You will notice that Aristotle departs radically from Plato in this. Knowledge of this world is possible without recourse to a permanent realm of Forms. On the contrary, forms or universals exist only in the things in this world, and knowledge consists not in the contemplation of Forms, but in getting one's hands dirty, examining and dissecting and poking the things of this changing world, coming to know their causes. In the case of the statue and other artefacts, form is imposed by some outside agency; while in the case of natural objects, Aristotle argues, internal principles direct the thing such that it becomes what it naturally becomes.

Of those natural objects which live – plants, animals and human beings – Aristotle's answer to the four questions of cause consists largely in the activity of soul. The soul, for Aristotle, is not something ghostly which inhabits the body. Instead it is, at least in part, the distinctive functioning of the body in question, what initiates its movement fixes its aims. To oversimplify more than a little, a plant's soul is vegetative, and as such it consists in growing; an animal's soul consists in this plus movement, appetite, and the power to sense certain things; a human being's soul consists in this, plus the power to think and know.

The virtue, or excellence, of a thing for Aristotle consists in the full development of the distinctive potentialities latent in its particular nature. An excellent plant, then, is one which manifests the full flowering (literally) of the plant soul: it grows very well indeed. An excellent horse is one which realizes the potentialities of the distinctive movements of horses: it covers the ground; perhaps its quick eye and attentive ear contribute to its fleetness. Excellence or virtue for humans insofar as we are rational consists in action in accordance with reason. This, Aristotle famously claims, consists in choosing the mean.

Choosing the Mean

Virtue consists in choosing the mean between two extremes, that is, in feeling and acting rightly given all the peculiar circumstances of a situation. If one faces mortal danger, Aristotle argues that courage consists in choosing the mean between the excesses of foolhardy rashness on one side and cowardice on the other. When one speaks about oneself, the virtue of truthfulness consists in choosing the mean between boasting and undue modesty. It is clear that Aristotle is not advocating what one might mistake for a Christian ethics of unqualified moderation. The mean varies from person to person and situation to situation. Thankfully, Milo the wrestler can choose his own mean when ordering the wine; an amount fine for him but excessive for the rest of us. There is nothing absolutist or exhaustive about Aristotle's notion of the mean: there is no mean when it comes to murder, he tells us. The best we can do is employ reason and decide on a case by case basis.

In what does the good life consist, given this view of virtue? Aristotle maintains that the good life requires friendship. Genuine virtue requires not only fellowship

MAJOR WORKS

We cannot say exactly when Aristotle wrote what has come down to us. It is likely that later editors made some changes and put the work in the order that it has now. Here is just some of it:

Nicomachean Ethics is among the most influential treatises on morality ever written. It contains a fascinating consideration of human happiness and virtue. It is perhaps most interesting for making the claim, forgotten by many later thinkers, that morality cannot be reduced to a series of universal principles.

Politics says something about the ideal state, which for Aristotle is one with the goal of well-being for its citizens. You will find here some disturbing remarks on slavery and the need for social harmony, which are partly mitigated by a consideration of the merits of democracy.

Physics is interesting for its consideration of the nature of explanation in what looks like budding science, as well as treatments of space and time. It also contains Aristotle's account of matter and form.

with equals, but sometimes self-sacrifice of varying sorts. Without friends, such action is not possible, and therefore a fully virtuous life is not possible. Friends afford the opportunity for goodness and happiness.

In addition, the full flowering of the intellectual virtues, the realization and exercise of our distinctive mental faculties, is required. Our rational capacities are part of what makes us what we are – just as a knife's capacity to cut makes a knife a knife. A good knife is one which cuts well, and a good human life is one filled with thinking well. A good life is certainly one in which we choose the mean, but it is also one in which rationality is given its head. Of the many goods we might aim at, the highest good, Aristotle argues, is the contemplative life, the life of the mind.

On with the Enquiry

This is, of course, only a caricature of the vast Aristotelian corpus. It overlooks many of the tensions, not to say outright contradictions, in his writing, and glosses over some very difficult technical philosophy. It is worth remembering, when we read him, that what we have really are works in progress, probably under constant revision throughout his life. It is difficult to imagine Aristotle satisfied with a treatise, content in the state of his own thinking on some matter or another, supposing, 'Well, that's all there is to know about that.' Aristotle was not so easily satisfied. Aristotle was also not one to waste last lines, and it is worth remembering the last line of the *Nicomachean Ethics* when faced with difficulties of interpretation. It is a long and bold treatise, dealing with more or less all thinking on ethics extant in Aristotle's time. He writes, at the end of what looks like a comprehensive account of virtue: 'Come, let us get on with the enquiry.'

Aristotle and his famous pupil, Alexander the Great, whom he tutored for several years before Alexander became king of Macedonia.

Marcus Aurelius

In his masterpiece, the Republic, Plato argues that the just state is ruled by the ones who know the Good, and at the top is the philosopher-king, a man born and quite literally bred to rule.

WHILE IT MIGHT BE TEMPTING TO THINK OF MARCUS AURELIUS (AD121–80) AS A PHILOSOPHER-KING, it would be a mistake. Marcus was a philosophically inclined Roman emperor, but not a philosopher-king in Plato's sense. Among other things, he did not undertake the rigorous programme of study required by Plato, and anyway, the philosophy Marcus espouses, though Platonic in places, is clearly generally Stoic in nature. However, it would also be a mistake to overlook Marcus, to take him for a second-rate thinker who happened to be an emperor. We have, in his writings, nothing less than a kind of distillation of Stoic philosophy that is filtered through the practical demands of someone in possession of monumental political power.

His route to power was unusual. Marcus was adopted and brought up well by his uncle, Emperor Antonius Pius (himself adopted by Emperor Hadrian). By all surviving accounts, Marcus was an excellent student of rhetoric, poetry and law, but he seems to have taken an early and very keen interest in philosophy, particularly the writings of the Stoic Epictetus. At a precocious age, perhaps as young as 11, he began to dress plainly and follow what he took to be a Stoic's severe regime of study, frugality and self-denial. Perhaps he went too far, because there are reports that his health suffered.

At a precocious age, Marcus began to dress plainly and follow what he took to be a Stoic's severe regime of study, frugality and self-denial.

On the death of Antonius, both Marcus and his worthless brother Lucius, also adopted by Antonius, ascended to the throne. It is clear that Marcus could have ruled alone, but remarkably he chose to offer Lucius joint rule. They shared power until Lucius's death in AD169. Marcus then ruled alone, and by all accounts generally well, until his death, possibly of plague, while conducting a campaign near the upper Danube.

If his death sounds unpleasant, it is nothing compared to Rome's troubles during his reign. He was almost constantly at war with Parthia; barbarians threatened at the northern borders of Italy; he spent years fighting German tribes along the Danube; he suppressed two revolts by recalcitrant lieutenants; his possibly faithless wife, Faustina, died suddenly; Rome suffered at least one major plague during his rule, as well as famine, floods, fires and earthquakes; and all but one of his children died young. His surviving child, Commodus, was vile and would not have been much comfort.

Writing the Meditations

In the midst of such strife, probably towards the end of his life, he wrote what has come down to us, rather miraculously, as the *Meditations*, which seems like his private diary. The work is manifestly not a standard philosophical treatise, with sustained argument for some well-articulated position. Instead we have a journal of disconnected musings, aphorisms and personal remonstration. The standard, probably excessively romantic view of the work is that Marcus wrote a few lines each night, at the end of a day's campaigning, during lonely vigils by a moonlit Danube. It may well be true.

Although Marcus was influenced by Plato, Heraclitus, the Cynics and others, it would be impossible to understand the Meditations without seeing it in the light of Stoicism, and in particular the writings of Epictetus. The Stoics were named for the *stoa poikile*, the painted porch or colonnade where they met in ancient Athens. The modern expressions 'being philosophical' or 'stoical' about misfortune come from their views.

Stoic Philosophy

The Stoics regard nature as itself divine and cyclical – the thinking is clearly pantheistic – consisting in cycles of life and cataclysmic conflagration, eternally repeated. The later Stoics concerned themselves more with ethics than metaphysics, and certainly the practical Roman mind of Marcus is preoccupied almost entirely with how one ought to live. Nevertheless, the view that nature is somehow both divine and heading in a certain direction, despite our choices, partially explains the Stoic's view that a life led in harmony with nature is the best life, the virtuous life. It also explains the Stoic's famously steadfast indifference to fortune and misfortune alike. Anything that happens to us is a part of the unfolding of a divine plan that is both beyond our power to influence and, itself, ultimately good.

A Stoic image which makes the point is of a dog tied to the back of a wagon. When the wagon moves, the dog can either be dragged yelping and barking and strangling itself by pulling in the opposite direction, or it can calmly go along with it. The dog heads off in the same direction no matter what it chooses to do; its only real choice being how it copes with its settled fate. As Marcus continually reminds himself, a Stoic must make a distinction between what is up to us and what is not up to us.

In this he echoes Epictetus: 'Up to us are opinion, impulse, desire, aversion. … Not up to us are body, property, reputation, office.' If you make the mistake of supposing, for example, that your social standing is up to you, within your sphere of control, you will be unhappy; you will take yourself to be harmed by those who overlook you for promotion and lament your failures. The failures, though, are not yours. You only have control over your opinions and attitudes, and here alone is virtue possible for the Stoic.

Our reactive attitudes to what goes on are up to us, but what actually happens in the universe is the unfolding of providence, itself good, but not up to us. One might rationally regard health, wealth and power as preferable to their opposites – the Stoic would consider them 'preferable indifferents' – but disappointment at failing to acquire such things as well as satisfaction upon their acquisition is pointless and irrational. Attaining such things is not up to us.

'Up to us are opinion, impulse, desire, aversion…Not up to us are body, property, reputation, office.'

Thus Marcus: 'Try living as a good man and see how you fare as one who is well pleased with what is allotted to him from the whole and finds his contentment in his own just conduct and kindly disposition.' A good or virtuous man accepts his lot, whatever it might be, and this follows from the recognition that whatever life the universe extends to us, it could not have been otherwise. The universe unfolds, and this itself is good, regardless of our myopic view of it. A good man is therefore someone who recognizes this, is pleased with whatever he has, and looks only to what is in his control: his reactions and his disposition. The good man harmonizes his inner life with providence.

The Problem of Free Will

Marcus lists one's conduct as something that is within one's control, and here there is a tension in Stoic philosophy which Marcus seems to gloss over. If things transpire

Contemporary work of Marcus Aurelius driving his chariot through the streets of Rome, possibly during the Triumph after the victory over the Parthians won by his joint Emperor, Lucius Verrus, AD166.

according to the universe's own plan, to what extent is our conduct up to us? A thorough-going determinist might press the point further: to what extent are even our opinions, impulses, desires and aversions up to us? The problem of free will emerges, and the Stoic philosopher Chrysippus, for one, argues that our actions are determined, but nevertheless our responsibility. Others dilute determinism, supposing that the broad strokes of fate will be drawn regardless, and our own inconsequential actions, though ours to choose, can make no difference to the big picture.

Whatever our view on free will, Marcus joins the Stoics in insisting that our reactions to things are what matter most. Pleasure and pain, health and wealth, power, glory and reputation are all nothing in themselves. Such things only take on a moral flavour when we judge them, when we take it that wealth is good and desirable, something to strive after. So Marcus urges himself to recognize that 'opinion is everything', and by saying this, of course, he means that opinion is nothing out there in the world. It is only our view on the world, and unless we are persuaded by Stoic principles, we can mistake our view of things for the things themselves. We can confuse our perception of harm, for example, when we are passed over for a pay rise, for actual harm. It is seeing an event as harmful rather than as an act of providence beyond our control that makes an event harmful. In reality, Marcus counsels, it is nothing to you. Nothing, in truth, can harm you but your perception of harm.

This is all very well, you might think, but the extra pay would have made a real difference to you: it would have made your life a little better. Maybe you could have afforded some more food and a new pair of shoes. It is clearly something more than 'nothing to you'. What is the difference between perceived harm and harm? Whether you perceive it as harmful or not, you are still walking around in uncomfortable shoes. Is the recognition that you have no control over the shoes you can afford, that your shoes are part of a divine plan, really much help when your feet hurt? You can press the point home to yourself by thinking not just of your uncomfortable shoes, but your death.

Marcus and Christianity

Marcus is aware of these lingering worries, particularly the problem presented by death. Part of the attraction of the *Meditations* is the opportunity it affords to witness someone working through the usual doubts which might trouble a person trying to live by Stoic principles. Marcus is nothing if not an honest thinker.

The *Meditations* has also been attractive to later Christian scholars, who see in Marcus a pagan struggling towards a view of life which finds full expression in Christian doctrine. Marcus's conception of providence, his modesty and temperance, his critical attitude towards his own imperfect virtue, his focus on the control of attitudes and desires: all these things are amenable to the Christian point of view. Ironically, it is clear that Marcus was no friend of Christianity, and he seems to have had a hand in the persecution and execution of Christians during his rule.

MAJOR WORKS

Meditations is the only work of a philosophical nature written by Marcus Aurelius. It is not entirely clear when the work was undertaken, though references to German campaigns and talk of his approaching death indicate to some that it was written late in his life.

Discourses, transcribed by his student Arrian, is a series of lectures by Epictetus, the Stoic who most influenced Marcus.

Saint Thomas Aquinas

Saint Thomas Aquinas (1225/6–1274) was an Italian Catholic philosopher and a major figure – if not the major figure – in the scholastic tradition. He gave rise to the Thomistic school of philosophy, for a long while the primary philosophical mainstay of the Roman Catholic Church.

THE LIFE OF THOMAS AQUINAS ended in a manner not quite befitting a saint and a Dominican friar (the Dominican brotherhood places value on a life of poverty and undertakes the begging of alms). He was born in his family's castle, the youngest son of Count Landulf of Aquino and Donna Theodora, herself with connections to Norman nobility. His education began at the age of five, when he was sent to the Abbey of Monte Cassino, and continued at what would eventually become the University of Naples.

A Devout Youth

It was here that the teenaged Aquinas came under the influence of the Dominicans, and when his noble family discovered that their son was about to join the brotherhood, his scandalized mother dispatched his older brothers to Naples with orders to abduct him, the aim being to hold him until he saw reason. He was kept a prisoner in the family castle for over a year. On one occasion, his brothers sent a prostitute into his room in a last desperate effort to break his resolve. However, Aquinas chased her out ith a burning stick from the fire. His family eventually despaired and relented. Aquinas won his freedom and joined the order.

In 1252 he went to Paris and began to teach. Eventually he took a Chair in the Faculty of Theology of Paris University. He spent the rest of his life moving between learned institutions in Italy and France, throughout it all producing a truly voluminous body of work – millions and millions of words – all the more remarkable given his short life. He had as many as four secretaries taking dictation: because of his astonishingly large output, his allegedly appalling handwriting, or perhaps both. The torrent of words stopped abruptly, however, when he had what he took to be a religious experience during mass. 'All that I have written seems to me like straw,' he said, 'compared to what has now been revealed to me.' A few months later, en route to a church council, he was struck on the head by an overhanging branch. He died shortly thereafter.

His enormous output was partly the result of his intellectual power and partly because he lived in remarkably provocative times. The works of **Aristotle** had

> *When a prostitute was sent to his room to break his resolve... Aquinas chased her away with a burning stick.*

recently become available in the West again, sometimes with accompanying heretical but persuasive commentaries composed by non-Christian thinkers of the stature of Averroes. Here were non-believers, reasoning well, who came to conclusions apparently in conflict with Christian teaching. The soul, they argued, is not immortal; the universe was not begun by a single, divine creative act but exists eternally; God knows only himself, not us. While some, at the time, were content to show simply that Aristotle and his commentators must be wrong, Aquinas wrote twelve commentaries on Aristotelian doctrine, arguing that Aristotle was getting at something like the partial truth. It was not just an exercise by him in Christianizing Aristotle, but a necessary step to combat heretical thinking.

The Influence of Aristotle

It was Aristotle's methods, as much as his conclusions, which disturbed the scholars of Aquinas's time. Aristotle claims that one must recognize the difference between what is to be assumed and what is to be proven before thinking can get under way. Knowledge builds on itself, and some disciplines nearer the top of the edifice are dependent on the truths below; they get going with assumptions grounded elsewhere.

Nearer the foundations of the structure are truths every rational person just has to accept if he or she wants to be rational. You cannot play the rationality game and take part in a debate, for example, if you do not accept the Law of the Excluded Middle: there is nothing between the assertion and the denial of a proposition. Only 'yes' or 'no' count as answers to questions of the form: 'Is it true that p?' If you do not accept that minimal requirement on rationality, you are doing something other than arguing; you have removed yourself from the debate. Assenting to some rules is just part of the warp and weft of rationality.

Aquinas draws a distinction between conclusions arrived at through reason and the truths of revelation. Obviously, the latter are authoritative for Aquinas, but (perhaps unusually for his time) he holds that the conclusions of reason in the writings of non-believers, Aristotle in particular, demand serious attention. Most interestingly, he argues that reason itself can arrive at some revelatory truths, and he sometimes adopts Aristotle's methods in order to do so. Further, his Dominican roots convinced him that one should stand ready to discourse on theology, particularly with those outside the faith. This means that premises must be sought to which even a non-believer would assent.

Perhaps this more than anything else explains the existence and tone of *Summa contra gentiles* (On the truth of the Catholic faith against the unbelievers). Next to his uncompleted masterwork, *Summa theologica* (Summation of theology), it is the best expression of his unusual attitude towards reason and those outside the faith.

Aquinas' Five Ways

An excellent example of Aquinas working with Aristotelian methods is to be found in his famous proofs of God's existence, the Five Ways or the *quinque viae*. Though their flavour might be owed to others, Aquinas's Aristotelian gloss makes his versions of the proofs remarkable. Each begins with empirical truths allegedly accepted by all and issues in the conclusion that God exists. We will consider just one, the Second Way.

Things in the world stand in causal relations. To use Aquinas's example, a stone moves, and this was caused by a stick which pushed it along, and this was caused by a hand, holding on to the stick, which moved it. Nothing, though, is a cause of itself; rather, causes are causes of other things, their distinct effects. An infinite regression of causal sequences is not possible. So there must be a first, uncaused cause, and this, Aquinas argues, everyone calls 'God'. In other words, one thing starts the whole chain going; one thing which is a cause but is not itself caused by anything else. Similar arguments are run for the existence of a first unmoved mover, a necessity underlying possibility; a perfection underpinning the gradations of the qualities of material things; and an argument for a God to explain the apparent order of the empirical world.

In each case, the argument runs backwards from empirical facts accepted by all – facts of motion, causation, change and qualities – to something responsible for the lot, something rendering intelligible the world around us. The arguments are open to many kinds of objection. One that most exercises philosophers takes issue with the move at the end of each argument, from the existence, say, of an uncaused first cause, to the existence of God: such and such must exist, and this we all call 'God'.

Why think that the uncaused cause has the many attributes we usually associate with the Christian God? Could there not be many uncaused causes at the back of the chain, rather than one God? Why think that the uncaused cause, if there is just one, is all-knowing, all-powerful and all-good? Maybe it is a rather pedestrian uncaused cause: without much in the way of rationality, only just powerful enough to get things rolling, possibly with malice on its mind. There seems to be something missing, perhaps a premise, between the inference from whatever it is which underwrites the causal sequence to that thing's being God.

If Aquinas thinks that reason can tell us that God exists, he maintains that it cannot get nearly as far with regard to knowledge of the nature of God. While we are naturally equipped to come to know something of the physical world, our capacity to wonder about the nature of God outstrips our ability to understand. We come by such knowledge as we can get indirectly, by analogy and by negation, and Aquinas maintains that this knowledge is imperfect at best.

MAJOR WORKS

Written between 1261 and 1264, Aquinas' major work was **Summa Contra Gentiles** (On the Truth of the Catholic Faith Against the Unbelievers). It contains long treatises on the nature of God, creatures, the end (the purpose, or telos) of creatures, and revelation.

Unfinished at his death, **Summa Theologiae** (Summation of Theology) is an enormous work, running to 60 volumes. It contains detailed reflection and argumentation which continues to shape religious and philosophical thinking.

What we can know of God

Much of what we can say we know of God's nature results from negating the properties of material things which we know better. We can say that God is not anywhere, not any time, not changing, not finite, and so on. We can also come to a partial, imperfect understanding of God's attributes by analogy with our knowledge of some of our properties. God is perfectly good, and we can know something of this by reflecting on what we know of goodness. God wills, and while this is a different thing to human willing, we can have an imperfect grasp of it by analogy to human will.

Still, there are things Aquinas claims can be known

about God's nature, though the story is a complex one. God's attributes are characterized by Aquinas as consisting in simplicity, actuality, perfection, goodness, infinitude, immutability, unity and immanence. However, our access to this knowledge and the character of the knowledge itself are special. Aquinas argues that knowledge of the divine nature, beyond mere analogy and negation, is possible only in virtue of God's intervention – grace or the beatific vision. Where reason falters, revelation picks up the slack. We might be able to reason our way to the conclusion that there is a God, but only revelation can tell us, for example, that God is a Trinity. Finite beings as we are, though, even grace cannot convey a comprehension of the divine, only an apprehension.

Aquinas's Influence

It is worth noting that Western philosophy, not just Western theology, owes a debt to Aquinas. It is possible to get the impression that Aquinas's concerns were just to do with the existence and nature of God, but that would be a mistake. His vast writings include considerations of human nature, government, law, ethics, metaphysics and epistemology, among a great deal else. In all of this Aquinas's influence has been large, both inside and outside the church.

Saint Thomas Aquinas standing between Aristotle and Plato and over the Arab philosopher Averroes. Detail from the Triumph of Saint Thomas Aquinas.

Niccolò Machiavelli

Born in Florence on 3 May 1469, Niccolò Machiavelli (1469–1527) is probably the world's best-known political scientist. His fame is such that his name functions as an adjective to denote cunning and unscrupulous behaviour devised to attain a particular end.

To DESCRIBE A POLITICIAN AS MACHIAVELLIAN IS TO SUGGEST that their lack of moral sensibility renders them unsuitable for public office. However, it is also to grant them a certain grudging respect; Machiavellian behaviour is associated with a particular kind of cool, calculating intelligence.

Machiavelli first came to prominence as a young Florentine diplomat. He secured his position as head of the republic's second chancery in 1498, at the age of 29. At this time, it was the custom in Florence for people occupying government positions to have had a strong grounding in the humanities. Machiavelli was no exception; his father, himself a keen scholar, had ensured that the young Niccolò was educated in the best traditions of Renaissance humanism.

The time which Machiavelli spent as a diplomat was essential to the development of his thought. Particularly, his ideas about effective leadership were rooted in a first-hand knowledge of the strengths and weaknesses of some of the major political figures of his age. Indeed, in his most famous work, *The Prince*, he made full use of a range of examples drawn from the real world, and in doing so, set himself apart from nearly all his predecessors. Machiavelli was interested in the grubby world of day-to-day politics.

> *This was something which Machiavelli was never to forget – serious politics requires strength, fortitude and the capacity to act decisively.*

Diplomatic Education

The lessons he learnt as a diplomat began almost immediately. In 1500, he was dispatched to the court of Louis XII of France to discuss the problems which had occurred when Florence, despite help from France, had failed to subdue Pisa, a rebellious city-state which at one time had been under Florentine control. The mission was beset with problems from the start. Though Machiavelli had little respect for the King of France, he was shocked to discover just how little the French thought of Florence. His native city was considered feeble and irresolute, lacking both the military and financial power to make an impact in foreign affairs. This was something which Machiavelli was never to forget; serious politics requires strength, fortitude and the capacity to act quickly and decisively.

This was hammered home to him shortly afterwards by the activities of Cesare

Borgia, who notoriously employed a ruthless cunning to extend the scope of his power after he had been made Duke of Romagna by his father Alexander VI. Machiavelli, who spent some time in the company of Borgia, clearly admired the way that he dealt with his enemies. In *The Prince*, for example, he relates with approval how Borgia used deception in order to lure the leaders of the Orsini, a faction which had been plotting against him, to the town of Sinigaglia, where he promptly murdered them all. Machiavelli leaves us in no doubt that he thinks that Borgia had many of the skills required for leadership:

> I believe I am correct in proposing that he be imitated by all those who have risen to power through Fortune and with the arms of others. Because he, possessing great courage and noble intentions could not have conducted himself in any other manner ... Anyone, therefore, who determines it necessary in his newly acquired principality to protect himself from his enemies, to win friends, to conquer either by force or by fraud, to make himself loved and feared by the people ... that person cannot find more recent examples than this man's deeds. (*The Prince*, Chapter 7)

However, despite Borgia's undoubted talents, his power did not last long. Mainly this was a matter of bad luck, but Machiavelli does criticize him in *The Prince* for helping Cardinal Giuliano della Rovere to become Pope Julius II, even though he had every reason to suspect that Rovere would not be favourably inclined towards him once he gained the papacy. In Machiavelli's view, Borgia relied too heavily upon his own self-confidence and upon the continuation of the good fortune he had enjoyed earlier in his career. In the end, this was the cause of his downfall; political leaders need to be able to temper their personality in the face of the particular situations they confront, and ultimately Cesare Borgia was lacking in this ability.

Machiavelli's diplomatic career, whilst providing him with the experience he needed to write *The Prince*, came to an unfortunate end in 1512. He was dismissed from his post late that year after the Medici family, having come to power in Florence, dissolved the republic. To make matters worse, a few months later he was wrongly accused of plotting against the new Medicean government, and then tortured and imprisoned. It was out of this turn of events that he came to write *The Prince*.

Machiavelli's magnum opus The Prince, *in which he sets out his idea of an ideal ruler.*

NICOLAI
MACHIAVELLI
PRINCEPS.

EX
SYLVESTRI TELII
FVLGINATIS TRADVCTIONE
diligenter emendata.

Adiecta sunt eiusdem argumenti, Aliorum quorundam contra Machiauellum scripta de potestate & officio Principum, & contra tyrannos.

BASILEAE
Ex officina Petri Pernæ.
M D XXC.

After he was released, he needed a way to ingratiate himself with the new Medici rulers. *The Prince*, the book which secured his reputation, was an attempt to show that he had abilities and knowledge which might be useful to a new ruler. The book's dedication says it all: *Niccolò Machiavelli to Lorenzo de' Medici, the Magnificent.*

The Prince

The book is primarily an essay on the art of leadership. It was first published in 1532, some seven years after the death of Machiavelli, and it was initially well received. However, it fairly quickly gained a certain notoriety for its suggestion that leaders should set aside moral considerations when making political decisions. Indeed, Machiavelli is considered by many to be an amoralist; that is, to have no interest in whether leaders behave morally, only in whether they are able to secure and retain political power and glory.

There is certainly an element of truth in this characterization of Machiavelli's philosophy. For example, he completely rejects the traditional conception – as outlined in Cicero's *De Officiis*, for example – which holds that the rational person, in order to achieve honour and glory, will always choose to act virtuously:

> …there is such a gap between how one lives and how one ought to live that anyone who abandons what is done for what ought to be done learns his ruin rather than his preservation: for a man who wishes to make a vocation of being good at all times will come to ruin among so many who are not good. Hence it is necessary for a prince who wishes to maintain his position to learn how not to be good, and to use this knowledge or not to use it according to necessity. (*The Prince*, Chapter 15).

This idea that leaders must learn how not to be good in order to rule effectively is rooted in a jaundiced view of the nature of human beings. Machiavelli thought that people were 'ungrateful, fickle, simulators and deceivers, avoiders of danger, greedy for gain' (*The Prince*, Chapter 17). As a result, certain styles of leadership just do not work. For example, Machiavelli argues that the prince who bases his power entirely on the love which the people apparently have for him is likely to be deserted when the going gets tough:

> …men are less hesitant about harming someone who makes himself loved than one who makes himself feared because love is held together by a chain of obligation which, since men are a sorry lot, is broken on every occasion in which their own self-interest is concerned; but fear is held together by a dread of punishment which will never abandon you.

There is then something right about the accusation that Machiavelli's ideas about leadership are predicated on a certain kind of amorality. However, this is not the whole story, for it is also the case that Machiavelli thought that effective leadership would often have good outcomes for everybody. For example, when considering whether it is better for a prince to rule by mercy or cruelty, Machiavelli argued that the excessively merciful prince, by tolerating disorder, will often bring greater harm to a community than the cruel prince who creates harmony through fear. Similarly, he noted that generosity in a leader will almost inevitably result in discord amongst the populace, because in the end the prince who is predisposed to lavish displays of spending will have to tax the people in order to pay for them, and will be resented and disliked as a result.

The Measure of a Leader

There is also a more general way that Machiavelli avoids the charge of amoralism. It was his view that a leader should strive for the goals of honour and glory. Indeed, it is a measure of a prince's *Virtú* that he is willing to do whatever is necessary in the face of unpredictable fortune to achieve this end. However, in Machiavelli's eyes, this does not justify cruelty for cruelty's sake; such behaviour might bring great power, but it will not bring honour and glory:

> Well used are those cruelties … that are carried out in a single stroke, done out of necessity to protect oneself, and are not continued but instead converted into the greatest possible benefits for the subjects. Badly used are those cruelties which, although being few at the outset, grow with the passing of time instead of disappearing. (*The Prince*, Chapter 8)

Machiavelli's hope that *The Prince* would propel him back into public life did not come to anything. Indeed, shortly after its completion at the end of 1513, he came to recognize that his career as a diplomat was over, and increasingly he reinvented himself as a man of letters. In the remaining years of his life, he became more and more sympathetic to the case for republican government. Indeed, his most famous text of this period, *Discourses on the First Ten Books of Titus Levy*, is a defence of republican government which takes ancient Rome as its exemplary model. In many ways, *Discourses* is the most sophisticated of his works. However, it is not what Machiavelli is destined to be remembered for writing. Rather, history, in equal measure, celebrates and condemns Machiavelli as the man who claimed that leaders need the strength of a lion and the cunning of a fox.

MAJOR WORKS

Niccoló Machiavelli only published two significant philosophical works, *The Prince* and *The Discourses* (Discourses on the First Ten Books of Titus Livy). However, interested readers might wish to have a look at *Art of War*, and also his collected letters.

The Prince (1532)

Machiavelli's most famous work is an incisive analysis on the art of leadership. It is argued that it is the primary duty of political leaders to secure and maintain power; and that it is necessary for them to set aside moral considerations when pursuing strategies to this end. It is this book which bequeathed the term 'Machiavellian' to posterity

The Discourses (1531)

In some ways Machiavelli's most sophisticated work, Discourses on the First Ten Books of Titus Livy is a defence of the principles of republican government, which takes ancient Rome as it exemplar.

Francis Bacon

Few philosophers divide the opinion of commentators as neatly as Bacon (1561–1626). Some have found early manifestations of the very precepts of the Enlightenment in his many writings, while others detect only anti-intellectual propaganda and a defence of the worst kind of religiosity.

1561–1626

BACON IS PRAISED BY SOME AS THE PROPHET OF MODERN SCIENCE, and identified by others as a buffoon whose only attempt at scientific experimentation resulted in his ridiculous death. He is currently reviled by feminists for, among other things, his alleged view that Mother Nature is there to be tamed and dominated, and hailed by students of Karl **Popper**, who find in his writings deep insights into the nature of what would become scientific method.

His life also is plausibly viewed from two competing perspectives. From one vantage point, he is a philosopher with a brilliant legal mind who rose to the height of power before his enemies toppled him with trumped-up charges of corruption. From another he is an unscrupulous self-publicist and social climber, gaining advantage for himself by any means until he is finally and justly ruined by his own greed.

Well-Connected

He certainly was born with advantageous family connections which he did try to use. His father was Sir Nicholas Bacon, Lord Keeper of the Great Seal, and his mother, Ann Cooke, was the sister-in-law of Sir William Cecil, Lord Treasurer. Following his education at Trinity College Cambridge, he was called to the bar and began a successful career in law. He combined this work with politics, joining Parliament at the age of 23. He was befriended by the Earl of Essex, who tried to help him by loaning him money and by joining Sir William in lobbying for Bacon's advancement at court. You can imagine the Earl's dismay when Bacon later successfully prosecuted him for treason on the orders of Queen Elizabeth. Despite Bacon's loyalty to the Queen, if that's what it was, and perhaps because of some injudicious remarks made about the government's taxation policy in a parliamentary debate, Elizabeth chose not to advance him.

Bacon saw in science nothing less than the possibility of understanding the natural world.

Bacon learned some sort of lesson from the Queen's displeasure and did all he could to remain in favour with her successor, James Stuart. James sought the conviction of a prisoner and thought torture and confession the only way to secure it. Sir Edward Coke, Bacon's rival, demurred, but Bacon obtained the conviction as instructed. His advancement quickly followed. He was knighted, made Attorney General, Lord Keeper, Lord Chancellor, Baron and finally Viscount St

Albans. It is difficult not to wonder about the hidden machinations responsible for Bacon's stellar promotion. It is this speculation which partly underpins the less charitable views of Bacon's life.

In the course of his career Bacon made enemies who eventually charged him with taking bribes. He admitted doing so, in some cases taking money from defendants in cases he judged, and the episode ruined him. He was fined the staggering sum of £40,000 and sent to the Tower. James eventually remitted the fine, released him from prison, and allowed him to retain his titles, but did not go so far as to pardon him officially. Bacon fled to the country but continued to write and reflect on both the law and science. In perhaps the most unfortunate death in the history of philosophy, the story goes that Bacon ventured outside on a cold winter's afternoon and stuffed a chicken's carcass with snow, perhaps experimenting with the notion that cold might preserve it. He contracted bronchitis and died soon after.

During the lean years, when Bacon was out of favour with Elizabeth, he wrote most of the fifty-eight essays for which he is duly remembered. The essays are entertaining and realist, perhaps Machiavellian – some contain advice to government officials on what we now recognize as spin-doctoring. However, it is *The Great Instauration*, the preface for six uncompleted works which together were intended to outline a programme for the restoration and advancement of human knowledge, for which Bacon is most famous. When Bacon wrote it, natural philosophy or budding science was more than a little hit or miss. Practitioners sometimes undertook bizarre 'experiments' simply to answer their own curiosity, and there was not much distinction between alchemy, magic and embryonic scientific enquiry. Bacon saw in science, if it was properly understood and undertaken, nothing less than the possibility of understanding the natural world and, in so doing, becoming master of it.

Idols

In this work, Bacon identifies the most pernicious obstructions (false idols) which stand in the way of an objective study of nature: the idols of the tribe, idols of the cave, idols of the marketplace and idols of the theatre. In each are claims which still echo in the halls of philosophy departments.

MAJOR WORKS

Quite early on in his career, Francis Bacon had declared to the world that he would concern himself with 'all knowledge'. He then announced that he personally would carry out nothing less than the complete reform and reorganization of human thought. Left unfinished at his death, **Magna Instauratio** or Great Instauration is Bacon's plan for this monumentally ambitious scheme.

Of the six parts of the work planned, only two were completed; the other four were left more as synopses than as any finished works.

De Dignitate et Augmentis Scientiarum (1623)
Part one of the Instauration, Nine Books on the Dignity and Advancement of Learning was published in 1623. Essentially a redrafting of his earlier *Proficience and Advancement of Learning*, the work outlines what Bacon regards as the principle obstacles to learning.

Novum Organon or **New Tool (1620)**
Contains what Bacon takes to be the methods proper to the interrogation of nature as well as the so-called 'idols' or impediments to truth.

Francis Bacon

The idols of the tribe are errors built into us as a species (the tribe of men). Humans see the world through human eyes, and such eyes are no sure guide to the real nature of things. Bacon has in mind not just the view that the senses are somehow fallible, but that humans are drawn into errors of judgement by an inbuilt, animal trust in sensory experience. Here too Bacon draws attention to something almost Kantian: that the mind imposes an order on what we see that is not really in the world. We are, Bacon argues, predisposed to order the world in our efforts to make sense of it, and in so doing we forget our active part in the order we find.

The idols of the cave are errors we are prone to as individuals, based on our particular preferences and agendas. What we notice in the world depends on our background of information: we notice what we are able to recognize and what interests us. One is no good in a dog-identifying contest if one doesn't much care about who wins, or has no idea what a dog is or looks like. Further, we overemphasize the importance of what we are looking for, what fits in with our aims or favourite prejudices, what slides easily along mental grooves long worn with use. Bacon's idea is that we are all imprisoned in our own theoretical frameworks, like the prisoners in **Plato**'s cave, and can be misled by the dim reflections of our own view on things. We end up just preferring a certain familiar view of the world, and it blinds us to other possibilities. Bacon warns that whatever one 'seizes on and dwells upon with peculiar satisfaction is to be held in suspicion'.

The errors of the marketplace arise as a result of human interaction, and here Bacon is pointing to problems in language. He has in mind not just loose or ambiguous talk, but the human capacity to talk past another person, with both parties none the wiser. Further, the fact that a word exists for something does not bring that thing into existence, Bacon argues. No matter how much the philosophers might go on about the Prime Mover, we have no evidence for the existence of the thing in the bare fact of our language use.

Bacon's invective throughout this discussion, it seems, is reserved for the idols of the theatre, and here he draws attention to the errors of traditional philosophical systems – no better than theatrical performances as guides to truth. While he takes issue with dogmatists who merely assert received philosophical opinion and the superstitious-minded who use philosophy to ground religion, his target is close to home: empirically-minded philosophers whose methods Bacon hopes to correct. Conclusions based on too few experiments, limited observation, and general failures of classification and method stand in the way of an understanding of the world.

A New Method

His corrective is something more than mere enumerative induction, the practice of observing particular instances and inferring a general conclusion based on them. He writes:

> [T]he greatest change I introduce is in the form itself of induction and the judgement made thereby. For the induction of which the logician speaks, which proceeds by simple enumeration, is a puerile thing … the greatest change I introduce is in the form of induction which shall analyze experience and take it to pieces, and by a due process of exclusion and rejection lead to an inevitable conclusion.

Bacon is advocating a methodical interrogation of natural phenomena in pursuit of more and more comprehensive laws, resulting in not just knowledge for its own sake, but power, utility, the control of things and thus the improvement of human life. It is much more than particular observations issuing in a general conclusion.

Bacon viewed every natural object as an amalgam of a limited number of simple natures or properties. By careful experimentation, one identifies and lists the many circumstances in which all instances of a nature appear (Tables of Presence), all instances in which a nature does not appear (Tables of Absence), and all cases involving an increase or decrease in the presence of a nature in the same object (Tables of Degrees or Comparisons). Suppose you are investigating heat, to use Bacon's example. You might note its presence in boiling water, its absence in ice, and you might see that it decreases as boiling water cools.

On the basis of exhaustive studies of the presence and absence of natures and comparisons of their varying degrees, one is able to formulate axioms, interpretations, or what we would now recognize as hypotheses, which then guide the choices made in further tests. One has studied the presence and absence of heat in the various states of water, and on the basis of this, one might hypothesize that other liquids behave in a similar manner. What about mercury? The next step is to boil some mercury and continue recording the results. In due course, perhaps after boiling a lot of fluids, it is possible to formulate a general law, say, of the behaviour of heat in liquids. The laws, Bacon argues, form a kind of pyramid of increasing coverage, and understanding and therefore control of things increases.

Of course, there might be a negative result, the hypothesis itself might be disproved, but this is still valuable. Bacon maintains that there are a limited number of natures and a limited number of false things to say about them. A negative result is in a sense better than a positive one. Discovering instances which support an hypothesis, even a very large number of instances, does not guarantee its truth. However, identifying falsehood amounts to a kind of certainty. True hypothesis have no false consequences, so a negative result is the only way to know for sure that a guess is the wrong one.

This is much more than the haphazard investigations that characterized 'natural philosophy' in Bacon's time. This is recognizable science.

The title page of Bacon's Magna Instauratio, *showing a ship setting sail on a voyage of discovery across an ocean of knowledge, a metaphor later used by Isaac Newton.*

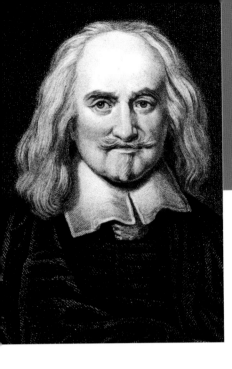

Thomas Hobbes

It is difficult to have anything but a great deal of admiration for someone who managed to annoy as diverse a group of people as did Thomas Hobbes (1588–1679).

1588–1679

PARLIAMENTARIANS WERE ANNOYED BY HIS CLAIM THAT THE KING'S RIGHT TO RULE IS ABSOLUTE, and Monarchists by his suggestion that the root of this power is not divine but granted by the people. Hobbes annoyed mathematicians by insisting in the face of overwhelming criticism that he had squared the circle. He annoyed **Descartes** by offering profound objections to his views shortly before the publication of the *Meditations*. He annoyed at least one bishop with his position on free-will and conducted a life-long public and sometimes acrimonious debate with him on the subject. He annoyed the Church by arguing, among other things, that the king is in charge of the interpretation of Scripture and atheists by taking the sacrament when he mistakenly thought he was about to die. Proof that a lecturer had indulged in 'Hobbism', a byword for atheism, was grounds for dismissal during Hobbes's lifetime. The possibility that Hobbes had annoyed even God was, for a time, seriously entertained. Following the Great Fire and the Great Plague, Parliament wondered whether Hobbes's writings had provoked God's retribution and were somehow responsible for London's disasters. A committee was set up which eventually demanded that Hobbes stop publishing.

Following the Great Fire and the Great Plague, Parliament wondered whether Hobbes's writings had provoked God's retribution.

Hobbes did not annoy everyone, however, and counted among his friends and supporters Gassendi, William Cavendish and at least one king. He was welcomed into the intellectual circle of the Abbé Mersenne, tutored Charles II, worked happily with Francis **Bacon** and exchanged views amicably with Galileo. And of course, he was concerned with more than just annoying people. He has been called, with some justice, the father of modern analytic philosophy, and he certainly ushered in modern political philosophy and social theory as we know it, breaking with traditional or mystical views of the origin of political power and turning instead to reason for its justification.

According to a story Hobbes himself did much to perpetuate, he was born prematurely when news of the approaching Spanish Armada frightened his mother into an early labour. His father was a vicar who fled the family home in some disgrace following his part in a brawl on the steps of his church. The young Hobbes was taken in by a well-to-do uncle, who saw to his education, eventually sending him to Oxford. Hobbes found lectures at university tedious, but following his

MAJOR WORKS

De Cive or On the Citizen (1642)

Perhaps the clearest and best articulated view of Hobbes' moral and political philosophy, despite the greater fame of *Leviathan*.

This book develops Hobbes' defence of the King's right to rule as an absolute monarch, first developed in *Elements of Law, Natural and Political* (1640).

Leviathan (1651)

Hobbes's philosophy undoubtedly finds its most complete expression in this work, his masterpiece of moral and political philosophy.

The book begins with an avowedly materialistic account of human nature and knowledge, as well as a deterministic account of human volition and free will. Its most striking content, however, is the pessimistic vision of the natural state of human beings it provides.

Hobbes regards this natural state as perpetual struggle against one's fellow man: it is in order to escape this grim fate, Hobbes argues, that we form the commonwealth, surrendering our individual rights to the authority of an absolute sovereign, who in return will ensure our security and well-being. For Hobbes, then, individual obedience to even an arbitrary government is necessary in order to forestall the greater evil of an endless state of war. The alternative to this commonwealth, Hobbes famously said, is a human life that is 'solitary, poor, nasty, brutish and short'.

Leviathan also has an often neglected second half, which got Hobbes into trouble, concerning the philosophy of religion.

graduation, he had the great fortune of becoming tutor to the son of William Cavendish, which gave him the the use of a splendid library and the promise of travel.

During his travels on the Continent, he discovered geometry and Galilean views on motion, and he put both at the heart of his thinking. Great strides could be made, he argued, by adopting a method owed to the proofs of geometry, that is, by beginning with small things and simple truths. Further, facts about human desire and sensation as well as large-scale human activities could be understood in terms of the motion of smaller parts. Laws not just of nature, but of human nature might be formulated. The bold culmination of Hobbes's thinking in this connection is *Leviathan*, which was published just after the execution of Charles I. When Hobbes returned from France, the powers in London were debating matters central to the book. Hobbes had a clearly articulated and highly relevant position, and his work was widely read.

Leviathan

The book is perhaps most famous for seeking a justification of political obligation through reflection on what human life would be without it, and Hobbes's conception of this state, the so-called 'state of nature', reflects a kind of deep pessimism concerning what it is to be human. The state of nature is characterized by both liberty and equality of a distinctly dark sort. Everyone in the state of nature has a share in absolute liberty, which seems to have two parts: it entails both the freedom to have anything a person can possess and keep as well as the freedom to do anything he can to preserve himself and what he has. A person has the right, then, to take any action 'to preserve his life' and 'do what he would … to possess, use and enjoy all that he would, or could get'. There is no such thing as a natural curb to human liberty, and Hobbes extends to the natural human even the right to kill. Further,

Thomas Hobbes' masterwork Leviathan. *The absolute ruler is shown watching benevolently over the land, armed with the badges of his authority, the sword and the sceptre.*

everyone in the state of nature is also equal in power, in so far as anyone has the capacity to kill anyone else: even the weak can, quite literally, club together and collectively overcome the strong.

People in the state of nature become enemies as surely as physical objects obey certain laws of motion. Goods, comforts and resources are naturally limited or scarce, and so competition for them is intense. Equally intense is what Hobbes identifies as 'natural diffidence', which is the fear or insecurity that characterizes natural human life – there can be no trust in the state of nature. The natural condition of human beings, that is to say, ungoverned human beings, is war, 'every man against every man'. You would not enjoy life in the state of nature, but you could perhaps console yourself with the fact that your suffering would be short as you probably would not last very long. As Hobbes puts it, in the state of nature there is 'no knowledge of the face of the earth; no account of time; no arts; no letters; no society; and which is worst of all, continual fear, and danger of violent death; and the life of man, solitary, poor, nasty, brutish, and short'.

The Laws of Nature

But you would want things to change. Perhaps the single, dim ray of light in this otherwise dark conception of what it is to be human are the three laws of nature that Hobbes identified. These laws of nature are dictates of reason, or conclusions one in the state of nature simply must draw. The first and most obvious law is that one must desire and seek the peace. Rationality, coupled with the fear of death, requires that people must wish to get themselves out of the state of nature, achieve better lives and some measure of security. Like a geometrical proof, the other laws follow on from this.

If one must seek the peace, one is then obliged to give up a share of one's natural right, one's liberty. Peace is not possible if everyone has an equal share in liberty, an equal right to everything and the means simply to take it. So Hobbes' second law of nature is that everyone gives up this natural right and is 'contented with so much liberty against other men, as he would allow other men against himself'. This consists in a mutual agreement amongst all those who seek protection, that is, a social contract, which in effect transfers absolute liberty from everyone to a single person (or group) who is then charged with using this power to keep the peace and ensure the security of all. As Hobbes puts it: '... it is as if every man should say to every other, "I authorise and give up my right of governing myself to this man or assembly of men, on this condition, that thou give up thy right to him, and authorise all his actions in like manner."'

Hobbes's third law of nature is that people must keep their covenants. But this rational requirement might not be enough, Hobbes notes, as covenants 'without the sword are but words'. To ensure safety from the horrors of our natural state, a serious sword is required, and Hobbes takes it that the power of the sovereign must be unqualified. The only sure way out of the state of nature is complete submission to a single, absolute power. The social contract, then, brings into being 'that great LEVIATHAN, or rather, to speak more reverently … that mortal God, to which we owe under the immortal God, our peace and defence'.

It is worth noting an important fact about this set-up. It is the people themselves who contract together – the social contract is not entered into by the people on one hand and the ruler on the other. Instead, the people make a 'free gift' of a part of their rights to the sovereign, and contract together to obey. Thus the king cannot in any sense break the contract, as he has not entered into it. However, reason demands that he avoid ingratitude, that he give the people no reason to 'repent him of this gift'. He is therefore obliged to make their safety the highest law. This might seem to you, rightly, as a thin restraint on the king and a thin basis for your protection. It has seemed to monarchists a little worrying too. Exactly what might happen should the people repent him of this gift? If the power of the sovereign rests on the consent of the governed, might that consent be lost or taken away?

The natural condition of human beings, that is to say, ungoverned human beings, is war, 'every man against every man'.

Criticisms of Hobbes

What seems to legitimize the absolute power of the government is the overwhelming desire to escape the state of nature. Hobbes's twin brother, fear, is at the heart of things here. Hobbes claims that reason leads us to the laws of nature, but it is fear of death and general insecurity which really warrant handing over liberty. It is worth asking whether fear really can lead us to the contemplation of not just someone who stands a chance of ensuring the peace, but a supreme and unlimited power. You might join John **Locke** in wondering whether this sort of thing is a good idea, even a rational course of action, for the fearful masses. If you fear even your fellows, can that fear be reason enough to create something monumentally dangerous? As Locke asks, a little incredulously, 'Are men so foolish that they take care to avoid what mischiefs may be done them by polecats or foxes, but are content, nay think it safety, to be devoured by lions?' Even if we follow Hobbes some way in his thinking about political obligation, it is not clear that we should follow him to absolutism.

But many have followed Hobbes, at least part of the way, maintaining that political obligation depends on some sort of consent, and social contract theory now has a long history of defenders. Some now take the contract to be implicit, adopting the old Socratic argument that enjoying the comforts and protection of the state is enough to oblige you to obey it, or in other words that it is as good as signing a contract. The philosopher John Rawls tells a story not about the state of nature, but the original position, from which he derives various principles of liberty and equality which are certainly not absolutist in nature. One wonders whether Hobbes himself might have found this annoying.

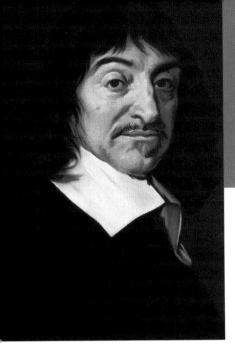

René Descartes

René Descartes (1596–1650) is the author of perhaps the most famous philosophical quote of all, cogito ergo sum, usually rendered as I think, therefore I am. There is however more to this quote, and more to Descartes' philosophy, than meets the eye.

1596–1650

RENÉ DESCARTES WAS REASONABLY YOUNG WHEN BURNING ASTRONOMERS seemed to the Church the right thing to do. Orthodox thinking at the time regarded the Earth as the centre of the created order, with the heavenly bodies – all perfect spheres – tracing arcs around the Earth in divinely ordained, circular orbits. Not only did Galileo see through his telescope moons orbiting something else, namely Jupiter, but he observed too that at least some of the planets were not themselves perfect spheres: they were bumpy, irregular, maybe squashed. Some looked a bit cracked and pock-marked – not at all the kind of shoddy work one expects from the Creator. Despite the Church's warnings, Galileo pursued all of this in writing. He attracted the attention of the Inquisition, which forced his public recantation.

It is hard not to think that all of this had a large influence on Descartes. So too did his formal education amongst the Jesuits of the Collége de La Fléche, begun when he was just 10 years old. The Jesuits promised clear and certain knowledge in return for diligent labour and careful study. As Descartes came of age, he found himself deeply troubled by uncertainty. He pouts: '… there was no such learning in the world as I had been led to hope.' If Copernicus and Galileo were right, how could we have gone so spectacularly wrong in thinking about such large questions as where the Earth is or whether or not it moves or what the planets are doing? In the midst of such embarrassments, Descartes found a single and remarkable exception: mathematics. He was more than simply a mathematical genius or prodigy, and his successes in it convinced him that its methods might one day be employed to secure truth in all other disciplines.

The Copernican View

He presented a version of this thinking in his first major work, *Rules for the Direction of the Mind*, and made use of it in a large scientific treatise called *The World*. In the latter, Descartes joins Galileo in advocating a heliocentric, Copernican view of the solar system, as well as the notion that humans might aspire to a godlike understanding of the world. It was published in 1633, the very year in which Galileo was nearly destroyed by the Inquisition. Descartes heeded the lesson of Galileo's experience and suppressed his book himself.

Four years later, he published anonymously the parts of the book on geometry, optics and meteorology, prefaced by what we now know as the *Discourse on Method*. It contains not only Descartes's rules for right reasoning in general but also the foundations of his epistemology and metaphysics. In a few short passages, Descartes breaks with more than a thousand years of thinking and ushers in the era of Modern Philosophy. The preoccupations, aims and assumptions characteristic of the following three hundred years of philosophy are largely those of Descartes.

The method is a generalization of Descartes's conception of mathematical demonstration. Even the most complex mathematical proofs are accomplished by a series of smaller steps – the truth of each, as well as nearby connections, are easily grasped. So too, Descartes argues, for all rational enquiry. Descartes encapsulates his method in four rules. (1) Accept nothing as true which is not presented to the mind so clearly and distinctly that there is no reason to doubt it. (2) Break problems down into as many smaller problems as possible. (3) Begin with what is most simple and easily understood, and build on this by degrees to larger and more complex matters. (4) Review the entire chain of thinking to ensure nothing is omitted.

Doubt and Knowledge

The first rule is probably the best known, as it is boldly expressed in the opening paragraphs of Descartes's *Meditations on First Philosophy*, perhaps the most important book of the modern period. Descartes hopes to secure a firm foundation for the natural sciences by establishing a first truth or truths. He does so by rejecting any beliefs which are open to even the slightest doubt, in the hope that at least one belief will survive and serve as a basis for further truths. The conception of knowledge operative here and in his other writings depends on a strict relation between knowing and certainty. If one genuinely knows some proposition, there is no room at all for doubt. Knowing requires certainty. Therefore, while the sceptical arguments of the first meditation might seem unpersuasive to one in a casual frame of mind, do note that Descartes is in pursuit of certain truth. If he finds even the slightest reason to doubt some belief or other – the most outlandish reason will do – the belief is no candidate for the firm foundation he seeks.

Descartes first notes that the senses can be deceptive, for instance, when one sees a stick which appears bent in a stream, and a wise person never trusts that which once deceives him. Ought we therefore never trust our sense-based beliefs? The argument cannot prove this much, not least because we would not be aware of illusions if we had no faith at all in sensory perception. We discover that the stick is not really bent by calling on the reinforcements of other sensory experiences; we feel the stick or take it

Descartes conducts a demonstration at the court of Queen Christina of Sweden, where he became 'philosopher-in-residence' in 1649 until his death the following year.

out of the water and look at it again. Descartes acknowledges this, saying that it would be a little crazy to think, just on the basis of the odd illusion, that he was not seated by the fire right now, writing in his notebook.

The second argument undercuts even this sort of everyday belief: one might be dreaming that one sees what one sees. Dreams, at the time of dreaming anyway, can seem just like waking life. If we have no criterion by which to distinguish being awake from being asleep, how do we know that for any belief we take to be true, we might not have dreamt its truth? Maybe your belief that your hand is holding this book is false. Actually, you are sound asleep, your eyes are closed, and your hand is under the pillow. The trouble here is that for any alleged criterion for wake-fulness, we can imagine the possibility of dreaming its satisfaction: you might dream of pinching yourself or waking up and realizing you were dreaming, and so on. Descartes argues that the dreaming possibility proves quite a bit. It casts doubt on all beliefs which require the world to be a certain way, and leaves us with only belief in the most simple and universal things: facts about bodies and shapes in general, place and time, and the truths of mathematics and logic.

These remaining beliefs are rendered dubious by certain reflections on our origins. We might have been created deliberately by God, who is certainly powerful enough to have built us to go wrong even with regard to simple and universal things, say something as obvious as counting the sides of a square. (If the possibility of a deceptive God is too heretical for you, Descartes offers the possibility of a malicious demon bent on your confusion.) Or we owe our existence to a sequence of accidental causes, in which case it is all the more likely that we are imperfectly built and again might go wrong with respect to even the most simple and universal things. The first meditation ends with Descartes contemplating the possibility that all his former beliefs are open to doubt.

Cartesian Dualism

It turns out, though, that one resilient belief remains. If deluded by illusion, led astray by a dream, or deceived by a demon, Descartes nevertheless cannot doubt that he himself exists. This is the first certainty of the *Meditations*, the anchor or foundation on which the Cartesian project depends: '[T]his proposition "I am", "I exist", whenever I utter it or conceive it in my mind, is necessarily true.' The Latin for this discovery, *Cogito ergo sum* (I am thinking, therefore I exist), is perhaps the best-known philosophical catch-phrase ever formulated. It is on the basis of the Cogito, as this first certainty is sometimes called, and in accord with his method, that Descartes attempts to build a series of additional truths.

The certainty, though, is a bare one. By 'I' Descartes means only a thing which thinks – which doubts, affirms, seems to see, hopes, and so on. His bodily nature and bodies in general remain open to doubt. This epistemological distinction is transformed by Descartes into a shaky metaphysical one, Cartesian Dualism: the mind and body are distinct things, different kinds of substances. Minds are things which think, and bodies are extended things, space-occupiers. The argument for the distinction depends on conceivability: it is conceivable that the mind can exist without the body; it is therefore possible that the mind can exist without the body; if such a thing is possible, then the mind and body cannot be the same thing. But of course conceivability is no sure guide to possibility. What we can conceive of depends on our background of theory and experience; it tells us something about our concepts but nothing clearly follows about the way the world is.

The distinction faces other problems too, perhaps the most difficult of which is the problem of interaction: exactly how can a thinking substance, which Descartes claims is not located in space, stand in a causal relation to a body, a thing which is located in space? This is a version of the mind-body problem, and twentieth-century philosophy of mind might be viewed as an attempt to struggle free of the concepts of mind and body Descartes has bequeathed to us. We have not yet managed it. We have many new distinctions and formulations of the problem – we have even contemplated some uncomfortable solutions – but it would be optimistic to say that we are much closer to the solution than was Descartes.

Whatever we make of dualism, Descartes follows the Cogito with further reflections, careful to assent only to that which is clearly and distinctly perceived, noting in particular the idea of a perfect God resident amongst the contents of his mind. Arguing that an effect must have at least as much reality or perfection as its cause, he claims that he could not simply have invented the idea of God. So Descartes is led to the belief that God exists and a conception of God as both a creator and a being without defect. Being deceptive is a kind of defect, and so Descartes reasons that God is no deceiver. If God is no deceiver, then we are not systematically misled with respect to those things we clearly and distinctly perceive, beliefs which survive our best and most careful scrutiny. It is a short step from here to the recovery of certain beliefs about the external world.

You might have noticed a tight circle in this series of reflections. God's goodness ensures that our clear and distinct perceptions are true; the proof of God's existence depends on such clear and distinct perceptions. The trouble is part of Descartes's legacy to us: beliefs seem easy to undermine but impossible to restore. Most commentators agree that Descartes's negative project of belief destruction succeeds, but his positive efforts to restore a firm foundation fail. Contemporary epistemology is, in large measure, an attempt to exorcise Descartes's demon.

MAJOR WORKS

Le Monde (1633) defends a heliocentric view of the solar system, and Descartes suppressed it himself, fearing censure by the Church.

Discourse on Method (1637) is the preface to *Optics, Meteorology and Geometry*, a toned down version of *Le Monde*. It is this preface which largely shaped modern philosophy, breaking as it did with Bacon's notion of scientific enquiry as well as Aristotelian thinking.

Meditations on First Philosophy (1641) might be the Modern Period's most important book. Certainly it put epistemology at the centre of philosophy and left us with sceptical problems we still deal with today. It lumbered us with Cartesian Dualism, the view that mind and body are distinct substances. It is also, of course, of interest to philosophers of religion for both Descartes' proof of God's existence and the role Descartes assigns to God in our efforts to understand the world.

Principles of Philosophy (1644) partly restates the metaphysical conclusions of the *Meditations*, focusing in particular on the relation of body and soul, but it also contains new material on the structure of the universe.

Blaise Pascal

Blaise Pascal (1623–62) was a man of many talents. In his short life, he made significant contributions to the fields of philosophy, mathematics, physics and theology.

WHEN NOT WORKING ON THE MYSTERIES OF THE UNIVERSE, PASCAL ALSO FOUND TIME to invent a calculating machine and to establish an omnibus system in Paris (the profits of which went to the poor). He is generally considered to have been one of the seventeenth century's best intellects; indeed, many commentators report that even the great philosopher René **Descartes** was envious of Pascal's prodigious abilities.

It was clear from a very early age that Pascal was going to be something special. His father Etienne, a trained lawyer and brilliant mathematician, with connections to some of the leading scientific thinkers of the age via his association with the Mersenne circle of natural philosophers, took on the task of his son's education. Blaise was extraordinarily precocious. His sister reports, for example, that by the age of 12 he had managed to work out Pythagoras's Theorem on his own. His father recognized his talent for mathematics and began to teach him. It was not long before Pascal was participating on his own terms in the discussions of the Mersenne group.

The calculating machine was a product of these early years. His father was working as Rouen's chief tax officer, a job which involved many routine, but time-consuming calculations. Pascal's machine, with its ability to manipulate numbers of up to six figures, was designed to remove some of the drudgery from the work. Although it proved to be too expensive to make to be a commercial success, it worked correctly, and it is generally considered to be the world's first geared computer.

Pascal was extraordinarily precocious; by age 12 he had worked out Pythagoras Theory for himself

Thoughts on Vacuum

Also at this time, Pascal was engaged in the scientific work which was to make his international reputation. He had become interested in a set of experiments by Torricelli which showed that when a tube of mercury was placed upside-down in a basin of mercury, a gap appeared at the top of the tube. The issue under debate had to do with what was in the gap. Traditional, scholastic thinkers, remaining true to the Aristotelian adage that nature abhors a vacuum, held that the tube contained some kind of subtle, invisible substance. Pascal's view was that such matters could not be decided by an appeal to authority, and, with Pierre Petit, he embarked on a series of experiments to determine the truth of the matter.

In 1647, after some four years of experimentation, he published his *Experiments on a vacuum*. In it, though he shied away from claiming definitively that the tube contained a vacuum, he outlined in some detail why the idea that the gap comprised a subtle substance was flawed. This provoked a response from Père Noël, the rector of the Jesuit Collège de Clermont in Paris, who remained committed to the traditional Aristotelian view. In his reply, Pascal set down what he considered to be the principles of scientific methodology, and in a move which in a way anticipated twentieth-century logical positivism, accused Noël of the invention, *ex nihilo*, of a substance which was, in principle, undetectable:

> If one asks them, or you, to make us see this matter, they reply that it is not visible. If one asks that it make some sound, they say that it cannot be heard, and likewise for all the other senses. Thus they think that they have achieved much by making others incapable of showing that subtle matter does not exist, thereby depriving themselves of any chance of showing that it does exist. But we find more reason to deny its existence because it cannot be proved, than to believe in it for the sole reason that one cannot prove that it does not exist.

Pascal further developed his thoughts on scientific methodology in his *Preface to a treatise on a vacuum*, which he wrote just a few years after his exchange of letters with Father Noël. In this, as well as reiterating his belief that appeals to authoritative texts and the like have no place in scientific reasoning, he outlined his view of science as a progressive enterprise, with new generations of scientists building on the knowledge handed down to them by their predecessors:

> The secrets of nature are concealed; although she is continually working, we do not always discover her effects: time reveals them from age to age, and although always alike in herself she is not always alike known. The experiments that give us the knowledge of these secrets are multiplied continually … It is in this manner that we may at the present day adopt different sentiments and new opinions, without despising the ancients and without ingratitude, since the first knowledge which they have given us has served as a stepping-stone to our own …

MAJOR WORKS

Experiments on a vacuum (1647)
Based on four years experimental research, this work argues against the traditional view that 'nature abhors a vacuum'.

Provincial Letters (1657)
A series of eighteen letters, which amount to a scathing attack on the views of the Jesuits. In essence, they are accused of expediency in their theological and moral out-look, willing to sacrifice doctrinal accuracy for the purposes of political gain.

Thoughts (or Pensées) (1670)
An apologia for Christianity. Unfinished at Pascal's death, this work comprises a series of short essays and aphorism. It is best known for featuring Pascal's famous wager ('Pascal's Wager'), an argument for the rationality of a belief in God.

Pascal employed a striking image to press this point home. He likened the learning of all men – in other words, scientific progress – to the learning of one immortal man over time. Learning is cumulative, and, in scientific terms, the ancients, our ancestors, were in their infancy. Moreover, it is fair to suppose that if the scientists of the past were privy to what we now know, they too would reassess commitments which were then held to be inviolate.

However, Pascal did not entirely rule out a role for authority in the quest for knowledge, for when it comes to theology, different rules come into play. In fact, according to Pascal, authority is the *only* measure of truth in theological matters; when we want to know about a realm which is beyond the reach of reason, then we have little choice but to rely on the authority of sacred texts.

Pascal's Conversion

This might seem a rather strange idea to be held by someone so committed to reason and evidence in the pursuit of scientific knowledge. However, Pascal, certainly in the latter part of his life, was a deeply religious man. Indeed, on the night of 23 November 1654, he underwent what might be called a conversion experience; it was sufficiently profound that he recorded it on a piece of parchment, which he then had sewn into his jacket, and which he carried with him for the rest of his life.

After this experience, Pascal turned increasingly to writing on religious matters. His *Letters Provinciales*, a series of 18 letters, published in 1656–7, was a scathing attack on the views of the Jesuits. In essence, he accused them of expediency in their theological and moral outlook; they were, he claimed, willing to sacrifice doctrinal accuracy for the purposes of political gain. The context of this dispute was a conflict between Jansenism, an approach to Christianity rooted in a strict interpretation of the ideas of Augustine, and the wider Catholic Church. By the time of the *Letters*, Pascal was a committed Jansenist; and his intervention in the dispute was an attempt to shore up support for Jansenism in the face of papal censure.

Pascal's wider theological views showed very clearly the influence of Augustine. He was committed to the Augustinian idea that the fall of man had left human beings spiritually corrupt to the core. It is only by the grace of God that people – and by no means all people – can be redeemed; in his view, God's grace is such that those people he had blessed will always choose to follow his path. However, as a good Augustinian, Pascal was also committed to the idea of predestination, that is, the idea that salvation is preordained. Therefore, there is nothing specifically that the individual can do to attain salvation; either God will make his presence felt in the heart of a particular individual, or he won't.

Pascal's Wager

This belief makes it slightly paradoxical that Pascal spent the final years of his life putting together the beginnings of an apologia for Christianity. Although it was never fully completed, the extant material was pieced together as *Pensées*. It is in this work that one finds Pascal's famous wager. The argument is as follows: either God exists or he does not. We have to choose one way or the other on this issue; it is an unavoidable existential dilemma. If God does not exist, then we lose very little by believing that he does exist. If he does exist, then we stand to gain an awful lot by believing that he does, and to lose an awful lot by thinking that he doesn't.

Therefore, it is sensible to wager that he does exist, and to behave appropriately. As Pascal put it: 'I should be much more afraid of being mistaken and then finding out that Christianity is true than of being mistaken in believing it to be true.'

The wager then is not an argument for the existence of God; Pascal was aware that he could not convince unbelievers of God's existence by rational argument. It is rather an argument for the rationality of *belief* in God. It was aimed not so much at people who were convinced that God did not exist, but rather at the waverers, people who were sceptical but interested. It does, however, sit uneasily with his Augustinian view of predestination. Pascal anticipated the criticism that the idea of trying to persuade people of the efficacy of religious belief is strange if it is true their belief is not constitutive of salvation. His response was that God might choose to do his work through other people, so it was his duty to attempt to bring people to faith. However, whilst this response might explain Pascal's motives, it isn't clear that Pascal's Wager can function as a motive to action. If a person's future is predestined, why do anything? Why not just sit back and wait for God to act?

Despite this difficulty, the wager has remained an influential argument. It is seen as an early example of decision-theory. Indeed, it is fair to say that amongst the educated public it is what Pascal is best known for. However, in a sense this is unfortunate; Pascal's reach was broad, and in twenty-first century terms his scientific and mathematical work is perhaps more impressive than his religious apologetics.

Early calculating machine designed and built by the young Pascal, to help his father calculate tax returns.

John Locke

John Locke (1632–1704) concerned himself primarily with society, where his views are often contrasted with those of Thomas Hobbes, and epistemology, where he is usually put with David Hume and Bishop Berkeley into the group known as the British Empiricists

IT IS WIDELY AGREED THAT JOHN LOCKE (1632–1704) IS THE FATHER OF MODERN EMPIRICISM, the view that knowledge comes not from innate ideas but experience. He is also undoubtedly a vastly influential moral and political philosopher, and some would go so far as to say that his thinking made possible the revolutions in both America and France. It is hard not to think of him as the greatest philosopher of the modern period in England – he did much to disentangle the philosophy of his day from scholastic and ancient Greek thinking. Some are willing to go further, arguing that he is the greatest philosopher England has ever produced. Certainly he shares a property with many others at the very top of the pantheon: those in power put him in fear for his life at least once.

Locke was born in Wrington, Somerset, to stern parents of the Puritan faith. His father arranged for his early education at Westminster School in London, where he eventually boarded, finally leaving to take up a studentship at Christ Church, Oxford, in 1652. It was at Christ Church that Locke began the odd practice of writing in codes and using invisible ink to keep his work secret. Many of Locke's papers and books were first published anonymously, and he seems to have been extremely secretive and suspicious of certain apparently blameless friends throughout his life.

Political Upheavals

He was much taken by the successes and the observational methods of what was then the new science, no doubt influenced by his colleague and friend at Oxford, Robert Boyle. His greatest friend at this time was Baron Ashley, who was eventually the Earl of Shaftesbury, who took such a liking to him that he made Locke his personal physician and quartered him in his London home. Locke assisted the Earl in a number of ways, and his friend seems to have had him appointed to several public boards. He became secretary to the Council of Trade and Plantations, which by all accounts he handled admirably and efficiently – he would eventually become its Commissioner. Locke was getting on well in the world.

His fortunes changed, however, when his patron became one of the leaders of parliamentary opposition to the Stuarts. Shaftesbury was tried and acquitted of treason in 1681, but given his close association, Locke feared that he might be in danger too. He was right. Locke fled to Holland in 1683, and James II insisted that the Dutch return him to England, possibly to be tried as a traitor. Little was made of this demand in Holland, but Locke was nevertheless forced to hide with supporters for a time. If his decade-long exile was sometimes harrowing, it nevertheless afforded Locke both the time and the intellectual stimulation he required to focus on two books he had been writing intermittently for perhaps a decade. By 1687, Locke was among the advisors of William of Orange, and when William was finally crowned, Locke returned, escorting the future Queen Mary. He was offered and took a number of posts, but devoted at least some of his time to completing his books.

Two Treatises of Government

One of these books, *Two Treatises of Government*, sets out Locke's political philosophy, and it is certainly a product of his times. The first treatise is an attack on the very idea of the divine right of kings, but it is the second which is most widely read. In it Locke argues that people living without a civil government in an imagined state of nature have certain duties to God not to harm the body, property or liberty of another, as well as corresponding rights to defend themselves, their property and liberty. In contrast to **Hobbes**'s claim that only an absolute ruler can save a person in the state of nature from the brutality of others, Locke argues that people form a government as a matter of convenience, designating a judge or set of judges to defend their natural rights. Although reason dictates that certain laws must be obeyed, not everyone has an equal share in rationality, and anyway it is possible for people to have reasonable disagreements. What is needed is a disinterested judge or set of judges, and this is the principle motivation for political obligation, for the social contract itself. In further contrast to Hobbes, the social contract is between the people and their appointed or otherwise chosen defenders. This makes possible a kind of contractual set of duties on the part of both the government and the people, and it has large implications. In virtue of their tyrannical conduct, for example, those in power might warrant their own overthrow.

In contrast to Hobbes, Locke argues that people form a government as a matter of convenience.

Concerning Human Understanding

The other book is *An Essay Concerning Human Understanding*, which Locke claims was inspired by a perplexing discussion he had with some friends while in the service of Shaftesbury – according to one source who probably was there, the topic was morality and revelation. They found themselves unable to make any headway and concluded that before progress could be made 'it was necessary to examine our own abilities, and see what objects our understandings were or were not fitted to deal with'. At the heart of this enquiry is the notion of an idea, because for Locke an idea is 'whatsoever is the object of the understanding when a man thinks'. What our minds are fitted to deal with depends on the nature of our ideas, and for Locke this question turns on how our ideas actually arise.

The first book of the *Essay* is an extended argument against the possibility that ideas are innate. This doctrine consists in the claim that the mind contains at least some ideas or principles which are not delivered by experience: some ideas are simply part of our factory specification. The view is first clearly expressed in **Plato**'s thinking, but it is evidently accepted by many of the schoolmen, as well as both **Descartes** and, with some qualifications, **Leibniz** in the modern period. Locke almost single-handedly derails this line of thinking.

William of Orange, the future William III of England and Locke's patron during his years in exile in the Netherlands.

The Doctrine of Innate Ideas

Locke takes it that the doctrine of innate ideas implies that there must be ideas or principles assented to by everyone, and he argues that there is no such universal assent. To use Locke's example, even a rock-bottom logical principle apparently required for reason to get off the ground is not assented to universally. 'Whatsoever is, is' might be such a principle, but the principle is not even known, let alone assented to, by 'children and idiots'.

It might be replied that anyone who is able to employ reason, or, in the case of a child, anyone who eventually comes to reason, will assent to such principles, and this proves that the principles are themselves innate, imprinted on the mind, waiting for discovery. Locke argues that this is no proof of innate ideas. First of all, it proves too much: it makes anything reason discovers, even truths of mathematics, innate. Second, even if everyone assents to some principle or other on coming to reason, this does not prove that the principle is innate. Another explanation or view of the origin of ideas fits this bill too. It is Locke's formulation of empiricism, his account of the opposing view, that is perhaps the best argument against the notion that some ideas are innate.

Locke argues that we are born with minds like blank tablets (*tabula rasa*), and experience alone is the source of our ideas. Ideas of sensation issue from our sensory experience, when our sensory apparatuses come into contact with the world, while ideas of reflection result from introspection, when we note the operations of our minds on ideas acquired by sensation. Ideas, considered generally, are of two types: simple and complex. A simple idea is 'nothing but one uniform appearance or conception in the mind, and is not distinguishable into different ideas'. Complex ideas are themselves composed of simple ideas. The mind is incapable of generating simple ideas, but it can furnish itself with complex ones by combining and shifting its store of simple ideas.

Primary and Secondary Qualities

It is easy to wonder about the relation between our ideas, the objects of knowledge according to Locke, and the real things in the world. Here Locke introduces a second distinction between the primary and secondary properties of objects. The former are 'utterly inseparable' from material objects; remain the same throughout all changes; and are a part of 'every particle of matter'. Locke identifies solidity, extension, figure, bulk and motion as primary properties of objects. Secondary properties, however, are 'nothing in the objects themselves but powers to produce various sensations in us by their primary qualities'. Here Locke has in mind colours, tastes, touches, smells and sounds. Our idea, say, of the shape of a lemon really does tell us something about the way the world is, but not so, or not exactly so, with the taste of a lemon.

Both the distinction between simple and complex ideas and the distinction between primary and secondary qualities have large implications for the limits of human understanding. At the end of the *Essay*, Locke's consideration of true and false ideas more or less outlines these limits from the empiricist point of view, and the fallout from his conclusions has been extensive. Locke maintains, for example, that there is a sense in which our complex ideas can lead us astray. We might combine simple ideas in such a way that nothing in nature answers to them. **Hume** argues that this is the case with such philosophical fictions as the enduring self, necessary causal connections and external objects – all are ideas which seem to lack a corresponding and legitimizing sensory impression. There also arises the question of the relation between our ideas of the qualities of objects and those objects themselves, which is a question pressed home by **Berkeley**. Locke's distinction between primary and secondary qualities requires that at least some of our ideas do not represent the way the world really is. It is a short step from here to wondering whether any of our ideas do.

Locke's Influence

Locke was much troubled in his lifetime by critics who thought that his empiricism could lead only to scepticism. However, with hindsight, we know that Locke's work led to much more. His thinking made not just Hume and Berkeley possible, perhaps even inevitable, but **Kant** and the tradition which followed him, not to mention the many manifestations of empiricism both within and without philosophy ever since. Locke's influence is evident most recently in the work of the pragmatists, the logical positivists and those those who argue that philosophy ought to be informed by the empirical sciences, philosophers who are hard at work in the present day.

MAJOR WORKS

Two Treatises of Government (1690) contains Locke's best political writing. The first treatise gives an account of Locke's critique of the divine right of kings. The second proposes Locke's alternative, the view that political obligation consists in the consent of the governed.

An Essay Concerning Human Understanding (1690) is Locke's greatest philosophical achievement. His aim in it is to determine exactly what the human mind is fitted to understand, and the book contains considerations of knowledge of the self, the world, and God. The book might be best known for Locke's annihilation of the doctrine of innate ideas. It gave empiricism a new start in the 17th Century.

Baruch Spinoza

Baruch Spinoza (1632–77) has inspired much admiration and affection from philosophers and students of philosophy alike: Bertrand Russell said of him that he was 'the noblest and most lovable of the great philosophers'.

THIS DID NOT, HOWEVER, AS RUSSELL WENT ON TO NOTE, PRECLUDE SPINOZA from being reviled in his time for his religious heterodoxy; indeed, as a young man he was excommunicated from his Jewish community for 'horrendous heresies'. The cause of his troubles were the unorthodox beliefs he held about God and the universe.

Spinoza was born in Amsterdam on 24 November 1632. His family were crypto-Jews; that is, they had been forced to adopt Christianity, yet secretly maintained their Jewish faith. His father, a successful merchant, had emigrated to Amsterdam in order to avoid persecution, and occupied a position of some prominence in the Jewish community. The young Spinoza was educated at the local Jewish school and synagogue, where he learnt Hebrew and Jewish theology. Outside school hours, he was tutored in Latin, German and some of the other European languages. Spinoza's father hoped that his son would choose to become a rabbi. However, by the time Spinoza turned 20, it was clear that this was not going to happen.

A Path from Judaism

Under the influence of Frances van den Enden, a private tutor, Spinoza had become increasingly dissatisfied with his rabbinical teachers, and had begun to identify with a number of unorthodox Christian groups, including, most significantly, the Collegiant sect. All this had placed his relations with the wider Jewish community under strain. Things came to a head in 1653, when he refused to repent his opinion that there is nothing in the Bible to lead one to suppose that God is without a body. After a 30-day period of excommunication, he was cursed and thrown out of the synagogue for good. On being informed of his fate, he reportedly replied: 'Very well. This does not force me to do anything that I would not have done of my own accord, had I not been afraid of a scandal.'

Given his treatment at the hands of religious authority, it is surely no coincidence that one of the two books he published in his lifetime was a call for religious tolerance and freedom. Published anonymously in 1670, the *Tractatus Theologico-Politicus* treated the Bible as a historical, culturally embedded document, which inevitably reflected the limited understanding of its authors. Thus, for example, Spinoza denied that the biblical miracles were supernatural in origin, claiming rather that they were natural phenomena which had been misunderstood by the authors of the Bible because of a lack of knowledge. Spinoza did, however, believe that the Bible articulated a consistent moral vision – one based on a message of love – and that it contained nothing to suggest that it supported religious intolerance.

Spinoza's *Ethics*

There is a certain irony in Spinoza's troubles with religious authority because it was his belief that God is literally everywhere. Or, to put this more accurately, it was Spinoza's claim that every existing thing is an aspect of just one substance, which is accurately described as God or Nature. He set out this view in his most famous work, *Ethics*, which was published by his friends shortly after his death.

The *Ethics* is a difficult read. This is partly because of the way in which it is constructed. Spinoza sets it down in a geometrical style, with rigorous, deductive argumentation from premises to conclusions. Indeed, according to Bertrand Russell, it is not worth the while for a modern student to learn the details of Spinoza's technical argument; it is enough to concentrate on the less formal remarks which appear in the notes and appendices.

Human beings themselves do not have a separate reality; they are simply aspects of the infinity of God.

Despite its difficulties, however, the *Ethics* is undoubtedly one of the classic texts of Western philosophy, so it is worth having a look at some of its arguments. In the first part of the work, Spinoza set out his metaphysical ideas, which rest on the notion that reality comprises just one substance, which, as indicated above, can be conceived of as either God or Nature. Spinoza argued that this one substance has an infinite number of attributes; however, it is only possible for human beings to know two of them, physical extension and thought. Human beings themselves do not have a separate reality; they are simply aspects of the infinity of God.

Immediately, it is possible to see how Spinoza's views came to be seen as heretical: God did not create nature, but rather God is equivalent to nature; and human beings are not straightforwardly the subjects of God, but rather aspects of

MAJOR WORKS

Baruch Spinoza only published one major work in his lifetime (*Theological-Political Treatise*). His outstanding work, *Ethics Demonstrated in a Geometrical Manner* (The Ethics), although completed in 1675, was not published until shortly after his death.

Theological-Political Treatise (1670)

This work treats the Bible as a historical, culturally embedded document, which inevitably reflects the limited understanding of its authors. The book was published anonymously as Spinoza was concerned, not without

reason, as to the sort of reception it could expect from organized religion.

The Ethics (1677)

Spinoza's major work, indeed one of the classics of modern philosophy, in which he sets out his metaphysical ideas, which rest on the notion that reality comprises just one substance, which can be conceived of as either God or Nature. *Ethics* was not published during Spinoza's lifetime, partly at least because he feared the reaction which its publication would provoke.

God. Moreover, Spinoza's view had implications for some of the standard themes of Christian theology. Perhaps most significantly, his idea that everything which occurs is simply a necessary manifestation of God or Nature allowed no room for free will, and consequently it rendered the notion of sin moot at best.

Spinoza was fully aware of this implication of his work. He claimed that people who believe 'that they speak or keep silence or act in any way from the free decision of their mind, do but dream with their eyes open'; and it is only because they are ignorant of the true causes of their actions that they are able to hold on to their dream:

> Experience teaches us no less clearly than reason, that men believe themselves to be free, simply because they are conscious of their actions, and unconscious of the causes whereby those actions are determined; and, further, it is plain that the dictates of the mind are but another name for the appetites, and therefore vary according to the varying state of the body. (*Ethics*)

Implications of the *Ethics*

The implications for ideas to do with sin and damnation are clear. If nothing can be other than it is, then what of moral responsibility? If the murderer has no freedom to choose not to murder, then it isn't clear he is morally responsible for his actions. And if everything in the universe is an aspect of God, then how can anything be bad or wrong? Interestingly, Spinoza's response to this question anticipated **Leibniz**'s treatment of the problem of evil. He argued that when viewed from the point of view of God, there is no evil in sin, since from the perspective of the totality there is nothing negative in sin; human beings only see evil in the world because they are unable to see how the whole of reality fits together. In other words, like Leibniz, he thought that our understanding of evil is distorted by our ignorance of the Divine.

However, it would not be true to think that Spinoza's system has no implications for the way that people should live. It was Spinoza's belief that the task for human beings is to see reality as God sees it, that is, from the perspective of eternity, or, in his words, 'under the aspect of eternity' (*sub specie aeternitatis*). To the extent that we are able to achieve this, we gain a kind of freedom; by recognizing our place in the larger whole and seeing its goodness, we free ourselves from certain of our passions, particularly those rooted in hopes and fears that are predicated upon human finitude. Thus, for example, Spinoza claimed, 'A free man thinks of nothing less than of death; and his wisdom is a meditation not of death, but of life.'

It should be clear why the arguments set out in the *Ethics* were unacceptable in terms of the orthodox Christianity of Spinoza's day. They were clearly contrary to many of the central tenets of the Christian faith, including, for example, the idea of the Fall of Man, the possibility of salvation and everlasting life through an acceptance of Jesus Christ, and the notion of God as the Father of Man.

Spinoza was well aware that the publication of his great work would earn him the opprobrium of the religious establishment. In fact, this occurred even without its publication, as he wrote to Henry Oldenburg, secretary of the Royal Society:

[A] rumour gained currency that I had in the press a book concerning God, wherein I endeavoured to show that there is no God. Hence certain theologians, perhaps the authors of the rumour, took occasion to complain of me before the prince and magistrates … When I became aware of this through trustworthy men, who also assured me that the theologians were everywhere lying in wait for me, I determined to put off publishing till I saw how things were going …

In fact, the book was not ever published in his lifetime. In 1676, Spinoza began to experience health difficulties; he had, for a while, been suffering from tuberculosis, which likely had been made worse by his work as a lens grinder. He died on 21 February 1676 at the age of 43. His biographers report that he met his death as his philosophy commanded, calmly and without complaint.

Spinoza enjoys a somewhat paradoxical reputation among philosophers today. His *Ethics* is recognized as one of the great achievements of Western philosophy, yet it is rarely studied in detail. This is perhaps because his metaphysics has largely been discounted; pantheism, the notion that God is in everything, has always been a marginal belief, and when it is combined with a smidgen of panpsychism – roughly speaking, the idea that mind is everywhere – it becomes even more marginal. However, Spinoza's ethical ideas retain their pertinence; particularly, there is something to be said for considering the travails of humanity from the perspective of the whole of reality; not in order to lessen our moral sensibility, but rather to help us to understand that we are but a tiny part of the universe. Bertrand Russell, in his great history of Western philosophy, suggested that in a painful world such reflections 'are a help towards sanity and an antidote to the paralysis of utter despair'. If he is right, then Spinoza's philosophy has something to teach us even today.

Moses parts the Red Sea and allows the Jews to escape their Egyptian pursuers. According to Spinoza, miracles such as this were no more than natural phenomena, a view which did little to endear him to Orthodox Judaism.

Gottfried Leibniz

Gottfried Leibniz (1647–1716), among his other achievements, invented differential calculus independently of Isaac Newton; much of the notation and vocabulary used today comes from Leibniz, who possessed a flair for both symbolism and language. He was also a pioneer in the field of symbolic logic.

1646–1716

> *My opinion is that God does nothing for which he does not deserve to be glorified.*

HOWEVER, IT IS THE MISFORTUNE OF LEIBNIZ THAT HE IS PROBABLY BEST KNOWN to most people as the inspiration for **Voltaire**'s satirical creation, Dr Pangloss, who spends his time in the novel *Candide* insisting that all is for the best in the best of all possible worlds, despite the fact that he is confronted with disaster after disaster. There is an element of truth in this characterization of Leibniz's philosophy – or his meta-physico-theologo-cosmolonigology, as Voltaire put it – but it would be a mistake to think that Leibniz was some sort of buffoon, since, in fact, he was one of the leading intellectual figures of his age.

He was born in Leipzig on 21 June 1646. His father, who taught Moral Philosophy at the University of Leipzig, died when he was only six years old, and he was raised mainly by his mother, who was careful to nurture and encourage his precocious intellectual talents. He taught himself Latin at an early age in order to read Livy, and then, having been given free run of his father's library, worked his way systematically through the ancients, Cicero, Herodotus, Seneca and **Plato**.

Leibniz went off to university when he was only 15 years old, first to Leipzig and then to Altdorf, graduating with degrees in Law and Philosophy. After receiving his doctorate in 1667, he was offered a professorship, but he declined it in favour of a diplomatic position at the Court of the Elector of Mainz. This decision was crucial to his intellectual development. In 1672, he was sent on diplomatic business to Paris, where he remained for 4 years, during which time he began to establish his reputation in European intellectual circles, meeting some of the leading thinkers of his day, including the mathematician Huygens, and the theologian and philosopher Malebranche.

During his time in Paris, Leibniz showed that he had wide intellectual interests. It was during this period that he laid down the foundations of differential calculus – independently of Newton – an achievement which would have recommended him to posterity even if he had done no important work in philosophy. He possessed prodigious ability in a number of separate fields. Like Blaise **Pascal**, he invented a calculating machine; he also designed various wind- and water-powered pumps which were supposed to drain mines (unfortunately, they didn't!); and he did significant work in geology, physics and even history.

Possibly because of his wide range of interests, his philosophy was never laid down in systematic fashion. Indeed, he only published one book in his lifetime – *The Theodicy* – preferring instead to set down his philosophy across a series of short articles and in voluminous correspondence. It is, nevertheless, possible to identify a number of key themes in his work.

The Best of all Possible Worlds

Perhaps the most important of these is the philosophical optimism which Voltaire satirizes in *Candide*. According to Leibniz, this world is the best of all possible worlds; to our modern minds – and, indeed, to Voltaire's not so modern mind – this is a somewhat implausible idea, but Leibniz thought it could be deduced from the terms of a rationalist theology. Put simply, the ontological argument shows that God, the most perfect being, exists; since he is perfect, it is inconceivable that he might have made things better than he has; therefore, this world is the best of all possible worlds.

Needless to say, this line of reasoning immediately raises a whole series of further issues. Even leaving aside questions about the ontological proof, there are problems with the argument. For example, it is possible that there is no best world, in which case God can only choose from an infinite series of worlds where each is better than the last. Leibniz rejects this criticism on the grounds that it compels God to make an arbitrary choice:

> For to think that God acts in anything without having any reason for his willing, even if we overlook the fact that such action seems impossible, is an opinion which conforms little to God's glory. For example, let us suppose that God chooses between A and B, and that he takes A without any reason for preferring it to B. I say that this action on the part of God is at least not praiseworthy, for all praise ought to be founded upon reason which ex hypothesi is not present here. My opinion is that God does nothing for which he does not deserve to be glorified. (*Discourse on Metaphysics*)

Perhaps more difficult for Leibniz's optimism is the 'problem of evil'. Stated very simply – though it has cropped up in various different forms – this holds that the evil which exists in the world rules out the existence of an all-powerful, loving God. The problem then for Leibniz is this: His argument is that a perfect God will create a perfect world; the trouble is that it is obvious that the world is not perfect, just consider the effects of the Bubonic plague, for example; therefore, by his own lights, there cannot be a perfect God.

Leibniz was aware of this problem, and had a number of responses to it. For example, he argued that it is simply a mistake to suppose that it is possible to eradicate particular evils from the world and yet leave the rest of the world unchanged. Thus, for instance, whilst it might appear to us that the world would have been a better place without the Great Plague of 1665, we are actually in no position to make that judgement. He also questioned whether human happiness was necessarily the right measure for assessing the goodness of the world. As an alternative, he suggested that the best world is the one which is the 'simplest in hypotheses and the richest in phenomena'; in other words, it is a parsimonious world.

The Best of All Possible Worlds: Leibniz's philosophical position was satirized in Voltaire's Candide.

Monads

It is not only in the area of theodicy that Leibniz's philosophical optimism makes its presence felt; it also makes an appearance in his famous metaphysical theory of substances. It was Leibniz's view, certainly in the latter part of his life, that reality is constituted by infinite number of unities or monads. These are simple, non-divisible, soul-like entities which lack extension, spatial position, shape, or indeed, any physical characteristics. Leibniz puts it like this:

> The Monad … is nothing but a simple substance, which enters into compounds. By 'simple' is meant 'without parts.' And there must be simple substances, since there are compounds; for a compound is nothing but a collection or aggregate of simples … These Monads are the real atoms of nature and, in a word, the elements of things. (*The Monadology*)

On the basis of this initial conception, Leibniz is able to deduce a number of other characteristics of monads. For example, he argued that they only exist and can only be destroyed by divine intervention; that they have no 'windows' through which anything can come in or out, so they cannot be affected by the actions of other entities, which means that they must be the sole source of their own activity; and that they are endowed with perception and appetition (the principle by which their perceptual states change).

What then of inanimate objects like computers, beds and books? Surely Leibniz didn't think that these were built out of monads, which, after all, he thought were soul-like entities? The answer is that he did; but out of 'bare monads', rather than the self-aware monads which are human minds. Liebniz's view was that monads are arranged in an infinite hierarchy; God, as the supreme monad, is at the top; human minds do pretty well, as a result of their capacity for rational thought and self-awareness; bare monads, only marginally percipient at all, come in at the bottom.

No doubt this all sounds very bizarre; not least because there is the question of how it is that it appears that things in the world interact with each other; given that Leibniz believed that monads are unable to affect each other, how is it that bodies, which comprise aggregates of monads, seem to do just that? It is here that Leibniz's philosophical optimism enters the picture. He argued that the regularities between monads were pre-established by a benevolent God; that monads were oriented towards each other in terms of a pre-existing harmony. To put this another way, it was Leibniz's view that God had created the universe in such a way that the actions of any one monad will automatically be reflected in the actions of all others.

Leibniz's standing as a philosopher took a while to grow. Partly, as it has already been noted, he was damaged by Voltaire's satirical treatment of his philosophical optimism in *Candide*; and partly the fact that his work was not published in a systematic way meant that it took a while for people to appreciate its full significance. However, with the publication of *New Essays on Human Understanding*, his book-length criticism of Locke's *Essay*, which was written at the turn of the eighteenth century but not published until some 50 years after his death, his reputation began to grow. Today Leibniz is recognized as one of the greatest philosophers of the seventeenth century. Many of the concepts and ideas which are now a standard part of the philosophical armoury – for example, the principle of sufficient reason, the identity of indiscernibles, and possible worlds – were introduced or foreshadowed in his work.

In common with a number of other philosophers, the last few years of Leibniz's life were not particularly good. In the aftermath of a row with the British scientific establishment over the originality of his differential calculus, he became embroiled in a bad-tempered correspondence with Samuel Clarke, a disciple of Newton, over the nature of space and time. Then, in 1714, his employer, Georg Ludwig, travelled to England to ascend the British throne but did not invite Leibniz to join him there, supposedly because he had not made sufficient progress with writing the history of the royal House of Brunswick. Two years later, on Sunday 14 November, Leibniz died in Hanover at the age of 70. He was buried a month later in an unmarked grave, which was hardly a fitting end for a man who had been celebrated in his lifetime as one of the seventeenth-century's greatest intellectual figures, and who would come to be recognized as one of the world's great philosophers.

MAJOR WORKS

Gottfried Leibniz only published one book in his lifetime, The Theodicy, preferring instead to set down his ideas in a series of short articles and voluminous correspondence. *The Cambridge Companion to Leibniz* is a good starting point to get a sense of this work; it also includes an essay by Roger Ariew, detailing Leibniz's life and works.

The Theodicy (1710)
Sub-titled 'Essays on the goodness of God', this work is primarily a defence of Leibniz's philosophical optimism as it relates to God. In particular, it contains a sophisticated response to the 'problem of evil'.

The Monadology (1714)
Not published until after his death, this is a short outline of Leibniz's view that reality is constituted by infinite number of unities or monads. These are simple, non-divisible, soul-like entities, which lack extension, spatial position, shape, or indeed, any physical characteristics.

New Essays in Human Understanding (1765)
Written at the turn of the eighteenth century, but not published until some fifty years after Leibniz's death, this work is a detailed, critical discussion of and response to John Locke's *Essay Concerning Human Understanding*.

George Berkeley

George Berkeley (1685–1753) was the philosopher who made the radical claim that all that exists are minds and the ideas in them. Famously mocked by Dr Johnson, Berkeley's theory is more sophisticated than it may first appear.

THERE IS A DISTINCTION BETWEEN HOW THINGS appear to us and how they really are. If you are in any doubt of it, stick a finger in one of your eyes just hard enough to double your vision. Either the act of sticking your finger in your eye resulted in the world quite literally doubling for a second, or something else doubled, namely, your perception or inner representation of things in the world. Once this distinction is obvious to you, and you realize you are not directly aware of the material objects in the world but are aware of them in virtue of inner representations or mental images, it is possible to ask all sorts of worrying questions. How do we know that our inner representations match the way the world really is? All we have are the representations and no way to climb outside our skulls and compare them to the way things really are. Worse, how do we know that there is a world out there at all? This is the philosophical problem of the external world, and it is not an easy one.

Perhaps the most radical solution to this problem is that proposed by George Berkeley, and it consists in the outright denial of the existence of a material world underlying our inner experience. It is not difficult to be sceptical about the existence of external objects, if you take it that minds and the ideas in them are all that exists. This is precisely Berkeley's view.

If his philosophical position is radical, his life certainly was not, and there is not much in it to explain why Berkeley developed his extraordinary line of thought. He was born in Kilkenny, attended Kilkenny College and Trinity College Dublin, eventually graduating and becoming a fellow himself in 1707. He was ordained into the Anglican Church three years later. It was during his years in Dublin that he formulated the arguments for his version of idealism, and he published the details in *The Principles of Human Knowledge* in the same year as his ordination. His position was almost instantly regarded as ridiculous, as proof of the madness of philosophers. Dr Samuel Johnson famously made sport of Berkeley by kicking a stone and proclaiming: 'I refute him thus.'

Quietly collecting himself, Berkeley tried again and published *Three Dialogues between Hylas and Philonous*, which patiently leads the reader through the motivation for the position and deals with objections to it. Though Berkeley's view is, to put it mildly, a little difficult to stomach, his writing is paradigmatically clear. The two books gained him a little ground – his easy and engaging personality gained him more – but he was welcomed into London intellectual life, perhaps as a kind of interesting curiosity. He travelled the Continent, became a fellow of Trinity College, eventually Dean of Derry, and were it not for the publication of a slightly bizarre book later in his life, the remainder of Berkeley's time on Earth would suggest nothing of his unusual thinking.

His *Siris: a chain of philosophical reflections and enquiries concerning the virtues of tar-water, and divers other subjects connected together and arising from one another* was published in 1744. This deeply odd book contains more than a little mysticism coupled with a serious consideration of the benefits of drinking water mixed with pine resin. Berkeley's *Principles*, probably the most carefully argued and best articulated statement of idealism ever written, was largely ignored in his lifetime, as were his treatises on vision and motion. There were six editions of *Siris*.

Ideas and Minds

Berkeley's arguments for idealism begin with a distinction between ideas and minds. All the objects of human knowledge, Berkeley argues, are either ideas immediately experienced through sensation – such things as the taste of my coffee, the cool feel of the desk, the visual images I have on looking out of the window – or ideas we have on thinking about our emotional states, or ideas we form through acts of memory and imagination. We give names to sensory experiences which cluster regularly together. Round, smooth, red sensations of a certain sort we call 'apples', and so on. In contrast to ideas, minds are active things: things which do the knowing, perceiving, sensing, willing, imagining and remembering. A mind is not one of our many ideas, 'but a thing entirely distinct from them, wherein they exist … whereby they are perceived; for the existence of an idea consists in being perceived.'

This last point is worth emphasizing. Ideas can exist only in a mind. The taste of a lemon cannot exist outside of a mind, but only in the act of tasting or remembering a taste. The way my shirt feels, its texture and tightness around my wrists, can only exist so long as I am feeling it. Feels and smells need feelers and smellers, minds to occupy, otherwise they cannot exist. These seemingly simple observations are more or less all Berkeley needs to get his arguments under way, and we will have a look at several of them.

The claim that, say, tables and chairs can exist outside of a mind is self-contradictory, according to Berkeley. Tables and chairs are things we perceive by sensation; what we perceive by sensation are sensory ideas (this chair feels a little bumpy, looks grey and black, makes a kind of groan when I sit in it); 'is it not plainly repugnant that any one of these, or any combination of them, should exist unperceived?' How could the feeling of bumpiness exist unfelt, outside a mind? The very idea of an unfelt feeling is self-contradictory.

Primary and Secondary Qualities

Stop right there, you might say. Plainly I have inner representations of things in the world, and some of the properties of these representations do depend on me, really are just in my mind. Something like the colour of an object really isn't in the object; light bounces off of the object and affects me in a certain way, gives me the experience of seeing red, say. I know the object really isn't objectively red, red whether I look at it or not.

Berkeley radically – and controversially – claimed that 'esse ist percipi' – that to be is to be perceived.

Maybe the bumpy feeling is like this as well. But there are other properties an object really has, like its shape or position or whether or not it is moving, and none of this is mind-dependent. This is an appeal to **Locke**'s distinction between primary (mind-independent) and secondary (mind-dependent) qualities, and Berkeley is having none of it.

He argues that the distinction collapses into nothing but mind-dependent qualities. One cannot imagine an object with primary qualities only. Berkeley maintains that 'it is not in my power to frame an idea of a body extended and moving, but I must withal give it some colour or other sensible quality, which is acknowledged to exist only in the mind'.

If what is allegedly mind-independent is itself inconceivable without something mind-dependent, the allegedly mind-independent thing is mind-dependent after all.

You might try admitting that the direct or immediate objects of knowledge are inner representations, but go on to claim that representations really do represent something genuinely external, a mind-independent reality. Our visual images, for example, are representative copies of real things out there in the world. However, Berkeley argues that 'an idea can be like nothing but another idea'. To say that our ideas represent the world or parts of it is to claim that, for example, a colour represents something out there which is itself never seen. Berkeley, almost audibly sighing, asks, 'I appeal to anyone whether it be sense to assert a colour is like something which is invisible.'

What then accounts for the regularity of our perceptions on Berkeley's view? If so-called 'physical objects' are ideas which exist only when perceived, what explains the fact that your sandwich is still there for you when you take it out of your rucksack? No one perceived it while it travelled to work with you, hidden away in your bag. Is Berkeley not committed to the absurd view that unperceived sandwiches wink out of existence when unperceived, only to reappear inexplicably at lunchtime? A materialist, someone who holds that matter really exists and underpins our sensory experience, has a quick answer to the reappearance of your sandwich: it actually existed all the while in the mind-independent world. Berkeley's world lacks a material substratum to underpin our perceptions. His solution to the problem is God.

The Mind of God

If ideas, including your sandwich, can only exist when perceived, then some mind or other must have kept your sandwich in existence by continuing to perceive it when no one else could. Not just sandwiches, but the whole world continues when we take our eyes off it, and it continues not just in any way, but in a certain way. There are patterns and regularities for us to discover in the natural world. No finite mind is up to the job of keeping everything in the world in mind. Berkeley sees, in the very regularity of our perceptual experiences, a proof of God's existence, even his benevolence. Thus Berkeley:

MAJOR WORKS

Principles of Human Knowledge (1710)
Berkeley's masterpiece and probably the clearest and best argued expression of metaphysical idealism in existence. In addition to arguments against materialism and abstraction, Berkeley makes plain the positive tenets of idealism, as well as a kind of proof of the existence of God.

Three Dialogues Between Hylas and Philonous (1713)
Guides the reader through the arguments for idealism in a dialogue form. It is a good thing to read after the *Principles*, as here Berkeley makes a deliberate effort to convince the sceptic.

De Motu or **On Motion (1720)**
A treatment of Newtonian physics in terms of Berkeley's own idealist views.

George Berkeley

Pulling rabbits from hats; the rabbit continues to exist when out of sight of the audience, according to Berkeley, because it is perceived by God.

'… every thing we see, hear, feel, or in any wise perceive by sense, being a sign or effect of the Power of God.'

This move clearly replaces one suspect thing with another. If Berkeley's arguments against a material substratum work by showing up inconsistencies or confusions or mysteries in the notion of substance, it will not do to substitute a divine mystery for a material one.

But Berkeley is happy with this sort of mystery. It is clear that at least a part of his motivation is a loathing of the cold, godless world afforded us by a certain conception of materialism. If the universe is nothing but matter in motion in space, there is not much room in it for morality and theism, and still less for the possibility that human life matters much in the grand scheme of things. In arguing for idealism, Berkeley saw himself as doing something about a dangerous line of thinking. He also thought his view was a remedy for scepticism about the external world, a restoration of the common man's beliefs. He maintains: 'That the things I see with my eyes and touch with my hands exist, really exist, I make not the least question. The only thing whose existence we deny is that which *philosophers* call Matter or corporeal substance. And in doing of this there is no damage done to the rest of mankind, who, I dare say, will never miss it.'

Whether or not Berkeley has produced a conception of the world consistent with the everyday man's outlook is an open question. Many, the mighty **Hume** included, read him as a kind of sceptic. However one characterizes his conclusions, it is clear, at least, that a reply to Berkeley must consist in something much more than merely kicking a stone.

Voltaire

François-Marie Arouet (1694–1778), or Voltaire as he is known to the world, was a French Enlightenment writer, deist and philosopher, whose importance lies less in his original contributions to philosophy, but more in his championing of reason in an age of unthinking brutality and superstition.

THE FRANCE INTO WHICH VOLTAIRE WAS BORN WAS BY TODAY'S STANDARDS – indeed, by the standards of most ages – brutal in the extreme. Its people lived under the yoke of an oppressive religious intolerance; to fall foul of the dominant Catholic Church was to court the most serious kind of danger. Jean Calas, a shopkeeper from Toulouse, found this out to his cost in 1762. For 40 years, he had lived a life of quiet anonymity with his wife and six children; then, one of his sons, depressed after his ambition to become a lawyer had been thwarted on account of his Protestantism, committed suicide. A rumour began that Jean Calas had murdered his son to prevent him from converting to Catholicism. Despite the absence of evidence, and Calas's previously unblemished record, he was sentenced to be tortured and killed.

Accordingly, on 16 March, he was tied between two iron rings and stretched until his four limbs were dislocated. He did not die, and continued to protest his innocence, so he was subjected to the *question extraordinaire*, which involved water being poured into his mouth until his body swelled to twice its usual size. His torturers, still unable to extract a confession, then bound him to a scaffold, smashed his limbs, and left him to die. Two hours later, finding that he was still alive, they took pity on him and strangled him.

At the time that this took place, Voltaire was at the height of his powers. He had befriended royalty, become a rich man through his business dealings, and gained an international reputation as a *philosophe* and champion of the oppressed. He came to hear of the Calas case and immediately moved to clear the dead man's name. It took three years, but after a campaign of letter writing, the publication of his *Treatise on Tolerance*, and the investment of a considerable amount of time and money, Voltaire managed to secure Calas's pardon. The great American secularist, Robert Green Ingersoll, reported that when Voltaire returned to Paris at the end of his life he was acclaimed by the crowds as the 'preserver of the Calas'.

A Champion of Reason

This story would be worth telling if it were about any of the great philosophers, but in Voltaire's case it is more than just an interesting anecdote – it gets right to the heart of his reputation. Voltaire is the most significant of the Enlightenment thinkers; he devoted a large part of his life to championing the cause of reason, and to exposing and pouring scorn upon the brutalities and absurdities of religious authoritarianism. He was the enemy of ignorance, myth and superstition, and, more often than not, it was Christianity which was in his sights. Thus, Ingersoll was led to declare that the name Voltaire inevitably excites the malignity of priests:

> Pronounce that name in the presence of a clergyman, and you will find that you have made a declaration of war. Pronounce that name, and from the face of the priest the mask of meekness will fall, and from the mouth of forgiveness will pour a Niagara of vituperation and calumny. And yet Voltaire was the greatest man of his century, and did more to free the human race than any other of the sons of men. (*Voltaire*)

Although there is little in Voltaire's background to suggest that he would become the eighteenth century's most notorious infidel, it is nevertheless possible to identify the seeds of his rebellion in his early years. His mother died when he was just seven years old, and, together with a fanatically religious elder brother, he was raised by his father, a devout Catholic. At the age of 10, despite showing no particular interest in religion, he was sent to the Jesuit college of Louis de Grand, where he later said that he learnt just Latin and a lot of nonsense. His father wanted him to pursue a career in law, but Voltaire had other ideas. In 1713, he travelled to Holland as an ambassador's aide, where he very quickly got himself into trouble over a girl, and was sent home in disgrace.

His father reacted to this episode by threatening him with arrest; under pressure, Voltaire sensibly consented to take a job in a solicitor's office. However, he did not stay out of trouble for long. The poems and epigrams he had taken to writing came to the attention of the authorities, and he was exiled to Tulle; on his return, he managed to get arrested again, and he was sent to the Bastille for a year (during which time he took the name Voltaire).

MAJOR WORKS

Letters Concerning the English (1733)
A key work of the Enlightenment, inspired by Voltaire's two-year stay in England. A series of short essays on politics, religion, philosophy and literature.

Treatise on Metaphysics (1734)
One of the few works of systematic philosophy that Voltaire produced. Heavily influenced by the philosophy of John Locke, it notably argues for a deistic position, in contrast to the more pessimistic view Voltaire would come to take in his later work.

Candide (1759)
A satirical novel which teases the philosophical optimism of Gottfried Liebniz, through the character of Dr. Pangloss, who holds on to the view that all is for the best in the best of all possible worlds, despite overwhelming evidence to the contrary.

A Treatise on Toleration (1763)
Written in the aftermath of the affair of Jean Calas, this work is a jeremiad against religious intolerance, and a plea for a brotherhood of humanity.

Philosophical Dictionary (1764)
A wide ranging demonstration of Voltaire's philosophical interests. Includes entries on free will, final causes, kissing and nakedness.

His life in France remained chaotic until he eventually left for England in 1726. He stayed for 2 years, and it was during this period that Voltaire began to engage in serious philosophical thinking. In his *Letters on the English* and *Treatise on Metaphysics*, both of which originated during this time, he showed that his thoughts had been influenced by his English experience. He followed **Locke**, for example, in rejecting the doctrine of innate ideas – roughly speaking, the doctrine that at least some ideas, for example, the idea of God, are not predicated on prior experience – which he identified primarily with **Descartes**:

> No one shall ever make me believe that I think always: and I am as little inclined as he [Locke] could be to fancy that some weeks after I was conceived I was a very learned soul; knowing at that time a thousand things which I forgot at my birth; and possessing when in the womb (though to no manner of purpose) knowledge which I lost the instant I had occasion for it; and which I have never since been able to recover perfectly. (*Letters on the English*)

The Nature of the Soul

He also adopted a sceptical and deflationary position on the question of the nature of the soul. He took the opponents of Locke to task for supposing that the idea of a material soul was necessarily an affront to religious sentiment. There was absolutely no reason to think that it was beyond the abilities of a creator with boundless power to transmit to our bodily organs those faculties of feeling and thinking which constitute human reason. As to the facts of the matter, Voltaire recognized that it was a controversial debate; certainly he thought that there were good reasons for supposing that people were composed of thinking matter; but, as for the larger question of the immortality of the soul, he was, in most respects, an agnostic – he regarded demonstrating the soul's immortality as beyond the abilities of human reason.

However, certainly at this stage in his life, there was interesting qualification to his agnosticism about the immortality of the soul. He was a deist – that is, he believed in a creator God – and thought at the very least that it was useful that people should *believe* the soul to be immortal. His early deism was providentialist in character; he argued that the universe displayed the marks of divinity in the order and regularity which Newton had so successfully explicated; and whilst he did not believe in an interventionist God, he nevertheless thought that God had created humans beings with the kinds of moral dispositions necessary for them to live good lives.

Voltaire was always aware that this kind of optimistic view was threatened by the presence of evil and suffering in the world. In his early writings, even if he was not able to deal adequately with the problem, he was able to deflect it, at least in his own mind. However, as time went on, he began increasingly to move away from this position; most particularly, he became ever more critical of **Leibniz**'s philosophical optimism, which held, roughly speaking, that this world, created by a rational God, is the best of all possible worlds.

His growing pessimism was reinforced by his experience of the senseless and arbitrary nature of much human misery. The Lisbon earthquake, in particular, seemed inexplicable in terms of an optimistic, providential deism. It occurred on

All Saints' Day in 1755 when the churches were full; 9,000 buildings were destroyed, and 30,000 people lost their lives. Voltaire used poetry to draw out the philosophical implications of the disaster:

> Come, ye philosophers, who cry, 'All's well,'
> And contemplate this ruin of a world.
> Behold these shreds and cinders of your race,
> This child and mother heaped in common wreck,
> These scattered limbs beneath the marble shafts –
> A hundred thousand whom the earth devours,
> Who, torn and bloody, palpitating yet,
> Entombed beneath their hospitable roofs,
> In racking torment end their stricken lives. (*Poem on the Lisbon Disaster*)

The Optimistic Dr Pangloss

His rejection of Leibnizian optimism found its apotheosis in perhaps his most famous work, the satirical novel *Candide*. The eponymous hero exists in a senseless world characterized by arbitrary and unnecessary suffering. Yet his mentor, Dr Pangloss, in line with his 'metaphysico-theologo-cosmolonigology', insists that all is for the best in the best of all possible worlds. As Candide moves from one disaster to another, he finds it increasingly difficult to accept Pangloss's optimism; and he is brought to understand the hopelessness of abstract philosophical speculation in the face of human suffering. The novel, however, ends on an upbeat note: it might be true that human beings live in a heartless world, but despair is not the answer; rather, one should engage in practical, efficacious action. In Candide's words, 'let us cultivate our garden'.

Voltaire takes the air with his patron Frederick of Prussia. Relations between the two would not always be cordial, however.

Voltaire is not a great philosopher in the sense of being a brilliantly original thinker. He is not a **Hume** or a **Kant**. His greatness lies rather in the role which he played in the emergence of reason in the face of myth and superstition, and in the eventual triumph of the Enlightenment. Even today, his name provokes strong reactions. He remains, for example, a focus of the ire of many people committed to biblical inerrancy. They'll happily tell you – falsely – that he died in turmoil, bitterly regretting his heresy. For other people, Voltaire is a hero; the person who above all others stood for the shining light of reason in the face of intolerance and bigotry. As Robert Green Ingersoll puts it, 'For half a century, past rack and stake, past dungeon and cathedral, past altar and throne, he carried with brave hands the sacred torch of Reason, whose light at last will flood the world.'

David Hume

David Hume (1711–76) was the greatest Scottish philosopher, without question. Probably, he was the greatest philosopher of the eighteenth century, itself a century of greats.

HUME MIGHT ALSO BE THE GREATEST MODERN PHILOSOPHER and the greatest empiricist; almost certainly he is the greatest philosopher in the sceptical tradition, a tradition perhaps closest to the heart of the impulse to philosophize. He is also the contemporary analytic philosopher's philosopher – promising graduate students are pointed to his work in the hope that something will rub off.

Hume was born in Edinburgh, his father's family a branch of the Earl of Home's and his mother's family a clutch of lawyers. Hume studied at the University of Edinburgh and was nudged towards the law, but he found an 'insurmountable aversion' to everything but philosophy, literature and history. He made up for his lack of funding by being frugal and industrious, and embarked upon a course of self-directed study. Whether or not this led to what some suspect was a nervous breakdown is unclear, but he quit his private researches and took employment as a clerk to a sugar merchant. Fortunately for us, he only lasted four months before being dismissed, and he then took up his studies again.

He moved to France in 1734 and wrote *A Treatise of Human Nature*; he came back to England with the hope of an excellent reception because of it. However, the book was almost entirely ignored. Hume laments: 'It fell dead-born from the press without reaching such distinction as even to excite a murmur among the zealots.' It was not, however, ignored by those who blocked his appointment to a professorship at the University of Edinburgh on charges of atheism and immorality. Hume never held an academic post.

There is a considerable difference between the perceptions of the mind and the later recall of those perceptions.

Hume, as he himself puts it, 'being naturally of a cheerful and sanguine temper … soon recovered' from his failure to attract interest with the book and published reworked portions of the *Treatise* in two slightly more digestible, smaller chunks entitled *An Enquiry Concerning Human Understanding* and *An Enquiry Concerning the Principles of Morals*. Again the British public were unmoved. (According to one commentator, it was likely that the only contemporaries able to understand Hume were Thomas Reid and Immanuel **Kant**. Both, arguably, spent their philosophical lives trying to deal with his conclusions.) Hume returned to France as assistant to England's ambassador, becoming a favourite in salon culture and something of a public figure. He published *The History of England* in 1754, and with it

Hume at last achieved the fame he had sought; unlike his philosophical works, the book was read widely and ran to six editions. His *Dialogues Concerning Natural Religion*, published posthumously, easily joins the *Enquiries* and the *Treatise* as being among the most important philosophical books ever written.

The Study of Human Nature

Hume's aims in his philosophical writings are many, but perhaps the most important is his hope that something akin to the Newtonian reductive explanation of motion might be achieved with regard to the study of human nature. His aim is to 'discover the secret springs and principles, by which the human mind is actuated in its operations'. His discoveries are entirely sceptical: what we take to be warranted or justified beliefs in every domain which matters most to us are, in fact, founded on something other than reason.

Hume operates with many distinctions, and we need at least three in order to get his arguments going. The first distinction is between impressions and ideas: 'There is a considerable difference between the perceptions of the mind, when a man feels the pain of excessive heat ... and when he afterwards recalls to his memory this sensation or anticipates it in his imagination.' The former are lively impressions and the latter are less forceful copies, or ideas.

The second distinction concerns the nature of ideas themselves: ideas might be either simple or complex. Following **Locke**, Hume argues that simple ideas cannot be broken down into still more simple ideas, while complex ideas are composed of two or more simple ones. It is important to note that simple ideas always have a corresponding simple impression in their first appearance, but this is not necessarily true for complex ideas. Thus, I get my simple idea of the taste of pineapple by tasting a pineapple, having the sensory impression. I might acquire a complex idea of a well-set table by looking at it. However, I might form my own complex idea, say, of a unicorn, by using my imagination to put together some simple ideas derived by impressions of horses and horns. I can be led astray into thinking my complex ideas correspond to something in the world, something experienced, when in fact they are mere fictions, products of the imagination.

The Five Ages of Man, from a baby to a skeleton. What, Hume asks, is it that endures throughout these changes?

David Hume

Facts and Ideas

The third distinction is between 'the objects of human reason or enquiry': relations of ideas and matters of fact. The former are propositions discoverable by the operation of thought alone, or armchair reflection. I can see the truths of mathematics and logic just by thinking about them, and in fact denying any such truth is self-contradictory. I can tell, for example, that $2 + 2 = 4$ is a relation of ideas because its negation or denial results in a contradiction. However, matters of fact depend on more than just thinking; I need to know how the world is in order to discover such truths. I need some experience to know that 'It's raining outside' is true. Simply negating the proposition leads to no contradiction, does not help me one way or the other. Hume maintains that propositions are only of these two types, and only the relevant sort of evidence corresponding to each can justify our claims to know them.

These distinctions and a measure of ingenious reflection secure Hume the following three disturbing conclusions: reason has no hand in our beliefs in the self, the external world or inductive inference. We will have a brief look at each.

On Causality

Suppose I claim to know that the president just resigned, and my evidence for this belief is a report in the newspaper I am are holding. What I am doing, according to Hume, is going beyond the present evidence of my senses (the newspaper) by thinking causally – taking the newspaper report as the effect of a certain cause, the resignation. Causal thinking is, Hume argues, the only way we can move beyond the narrow band of present sensory experience, from the observed to the unobserved, from the present to the past and the future. Having had lots of experiences in the past of particular causes (political events) issuing in particular effects (newspaper reports) I expect that this cause-effect conjunction will continue to hold, and that the effect I see now is caused in the same reliable way as the past effects I have seen. What underpins our inference is the Principle of Induction: the future will be like the past. But, Hume asks, what justifies our belief in this principle?

The principle cannot be a relation of ideas, as its negation – the future will not be like the past – is perfectly conceivable, not self-contradictory. Nor can the principle be justified in terms of matters of fact, the truths discovered by experience, as this would be circular. We would be arguing that the future will be like the past, because in the past the future was like the past. This amounts to using induction to prove the principle of induction, and it is no justification. Instead of reason, Hume argues, custom or habit leads us to expect like causes to produce like effects. At bottom, nothing but human nature underpins our thinking in this connection.

What about our belief in an enduring self, the belief that we are persons or selves who persist over time? I think, when I see a photo of myself as a baby, that I'm looking at a picture of an earlier version of me. I also think, in a spirit of optimism, that I will still be that person for maybe 20 more years or so. There must be something, the self, that endures through all the changes and makes me *me*. Hume admits that we have this idea, but to be a genuine idea it must come from some impression. Yet when he looks inwards, introspects, he finds no unchanging impression to legitimize the idea. All he discovers is a constantly changing bundle of perceptions, but no enduring self. Hume concludes that the notion of a self is a fictitious product of the imagination.

Scepticism

Where do we arrive at the notion of objects which continue to exist distinct from our minds, the occupants of the external world in other words? It is plainly impossible to arrive at this idea from sensation, as this would involve us in the absurdity of claiming that we have sensory impressions of objects which continue to exist when we do not sense them. Among other things, Hume points to **Berkeley** for a critique of the possibility that reason delivers the idea. If not sensation and reason, what else but the imagination could lead us to think that enduring objects exist?

It is not clear what to make of Hume's sceptical view of human rationality. Hume himself feels the tension, sometimes admitting that his conclusions have no force when he withdraws from his study and gets about the business of living. Elsewhere, though, what he thinks follows from his philosophy is clear enough. In this passage, Hume as librarian considers the worth of books about anything other than mathematics (abstract reasoning) or the reports of sensation (experimental reasoning). He writes:

> When we run over libraries, persuaded of these principles, what havoc must we make? If we take in our hand any volume; of divinity or school metaphysics, for instance, let us ask, *Does it contain any abstract reasoning concerning quantity or number?* No. *Does it contain any experimental reasoning concerning matter of fact and existence?* No. Commit it then to the flames: for it can contain nothing but sophistry and illusion.

We probably do not yet know the full implications of Hume's thinking because we are still catching up with him. What is depressing is that Hume might have left much more philosophy in the world had things been a little different. Had Hume been widely read and understood in his lifetime, he might have produced a great deal in response to criticism and questioning. It is hard not to regret philosophy's loss.

MAJOR WORKS

Treatise of Human Nature (1739)

Largely neglected in Hume's lifetime, but it is clearly one of the greatest and most important philosophy books ever written. Divided into three parts – on the understanding, the passions and morals – it was intended as nothing less than a complete analysis of human nature.

An Enquiry Concerning Human Understanding (1748)

A shortened and more accessible version of book one of the *Treatise* and is probably the most interesting of Hume's shorter works. It contains his formulation of the problem of induction, speculation on causal necessity, a spectacular argument against belief in miracles, as well as instructive thoughts on the nature of scepticism, along with much else.

An Enquiry Concerning the Principles of Morals (1751)

Hume's attempt to found a system of morality not on religious doctrine but on utility and sentiment.

Dialogues Concerning Natural Religion (1779)

Considered so controversial that it was published three years after Hume's death and did not include the publisher's name. It contains a series of brilliant objections to more or less all of the largest arguments for the existence of God.

Jean-Jacques Rousseau

Jean-Jacques Rousseau (1712–78) rose from humble beginnings to become a leading figure of the 18th-century French Enlightenment, alongside such giants as Diderot and Voltaire.

1712–78

ROUSSEAU LIVED A LIFE WHICH WAS AS COLOURFUL AS THE LIVES of any of the great philosophers. He was born in Geneva, the son of Isaac Rousseau, a watchmaker. His mother, Susannah Bernard, died very soon after his birth, and for the first 10 years of his life he was raised by his father. It was during this time that he was introduced to the delights of literature. In his *Confessions*, he reported that he would sometimes spend all night with his father reading the romance novels which had been part of a collection of his mother's, an activity which he said resulted in an early interest in the passions. After 1719, he gravitated to more serious works, including Plutarch's *Lives* and Ovid's *Metamorphoses*.

These early years were very important for the development of his later political and social ideas. For example, his commitment to liberty and his sympathy for republican ideals had their roots in this period:

> Incessantly occupied with Rome and Athens, conversing, if I may so express myself, with their illustrious heroes; born the citizen of a republic, of a father whose ruling passion was the love of his country, I was fired with these examples; could fancy myself a Greek or Roman, and readily give into the character of the personage whose life I read; transported by the recital of any extraordinary instance of fortitude or intrepidity, animation flashed from my eyes, and gave my voice additional strength and energy. (*Confessions*)

In 1722, however, things changed for Rousseau; his father elected to leave Geneva as an alternative to imprisonment, after getting involved in a brawl; and Jean-Jacques was sent with his cousin to live in Bossey, a village not too far from their home town. He returned two years later to live with his uncle in Geneva, and then spent an unhappy and rather brutal period as an apprentice engraver. He eventually fled this situation, and on the advice of a Father de Pontverre sought out Madame de Warens, who had gained something of a reputation for securing Catholic converts, and entered her care. This was to be the making of him. Over the next 10 years, he completed his education, discovered a passion for music, started to think in terms of a career as a man of letters, and in 1733, somewhat reluctantly, became Madame de Warens's lover.

This relationship did not last, and in 1742 Rousseau moved to Paris. If meeting de Warens had been the turning point of his youth, then this was the turning point of his adulthood. Quite soon after his arrival, having befriended the *encyclopédist* Diderot, he began to establish a reputation in Parisian intellectual circles. This exploded in 1750 on the publication of his first major work, *Discourse on the Sciences and Art*, which he wrote as an entry to a competition – which he subsequently won – which had posed the question whether advancements in the sciences and arts had improved morals. In comparison with his later works, the thesis Rousseau advances in this essay is rather naive. However, it does set out what is perhaps the central contention of his life's work; namely, that the advent of civilization has in certain ways corrupted the natural goodness of human beings.

On Progress

His specific argument in this essay is that progress in the arts and sciences has always been accompanied by moral degeneration; sophistication in these realms is a function of idleness and a predilection for luxury, and it contributes to the decay of those societies where it is most marked. Thus, for example, as soon as Egypt, Athens and Rome reached a certain level of cultural sophistication, decadence inevitably set in, and it wasn't long before they fell under the yoke of foreign powers. Rousseau recognizes that there will always be a few celebrated people able to make genuine contributions to humanity's fortunes; but as for the rest of us: '... let us remain in our obscurity. Let us not covet a reputation we should never attain, and which, in the present state of things, would never make up to us for the trouble it would have cost us, even if we were fully qualified to obtain it' (*Discourse on the Sciences and Art*).

The Triumph of Reason and Truth; *philosophy, in the form of Jean-Jacques Rousseau, uncovers reason and truth, hidden from the universe by error and lies, in this late eighteenth century engraving.*

The publication of this essay created a bit of a storm in French intellectual circles. It was perceived as a counterblast against the Enlightenment idea that the best hope for the betterment of humankind is the progress which occurs as societies throw off the vestiges of a past dominated by superstition and myth. Rousseau just didn't, in any straightforward sense, accept this idea, which became absolutely apparent with the publication of his second discourse on the origins of inequality.

In the first part of this he set out his idea of the 'noble savage', or 'savage man', who lives a solitary, peaceable existence concerned mainly with the fulfilment of immediate needs, and having little use for foresight, language or any of the other things which come with a social existence. This idea stood in marked contrast with those of philosophers like **Hobbes**, who saw the life of man in a state of nature as nasty, brutish and short. And, of course, that was the point; for it was Rousseau's intent to show that the vices of human beings exist because people live in social groups; and that as inequality inevitably emerges and then increases, so they are magnified.

Rousseau is not wholly clear about how 'savage man' originally departed from a solitary life in a state of nature. He alludes to increases in population and the advantages of minimal co-operation in difficult times. However, what is certain is that once people began to enjoy fixed relations with each other, the conditions were ripe for the emergence of competitiveness, jealousy and aggression:

> Everyone begins to survey the rest, and wishes to be surveyed himself; and public esteem acquires a value. He who sings or dances best; the handsomest, the strongest...the most eloquent, comes to be the most respected: this was the first step towards inequality, and at the same time towards vice. From these first preferences there proceeded on one side vanity and contempt, on the other envy and shame; and the fermentation raised by these new leavens at length produced combinations fatal to happiness and innocence. (*Discourse on the Origins and Foundations of Inequality*)

In Rousseau's view, even this situation would have been comparatively benign were it not for the emergence of private property. Indeed, Rousseau argues that civil society was effectively founded by the person who first enclosed and then claimed ownership over a piece of land; once there were people simple enough to believe the claim, civil society, as a means of justifying and maintaining property relations – that is, relations of inequality – was inevitable. At root, then, private property lies at the heart of inequality, and its associated moral turpitude.

The Social Contract

Rousseau did not think that it was possible for humankind to return to a state of nature (indeed, he thought it likely that a state of nature never existed in precisely the form he specified). This, of course, leaves a problem: how are humans best to

MAJOR WORKS

Discourse on the Sciences and Art (1750)

The winning entry to an essay competition, it catapulted Rousseau to fame. Although clearly an immature work, its thesis that the advent of civilisation has in certain ways corrupted the natural goodness of human beings proved highly contentious.

Discourse on the Origin of Inequality (1755)

An important critique of the ideas of philosophers such as Locke, this essay set down the idea that private property was the major source of the moral ills of modern societies.

The Social Contract (1762)

Generally, though not universally, considered to be Rousseau's masterpiece. It sets out the argument that sovereignty should express the general will of the social body, requiring that individuals when acting as members of that body set aside their own personal, sectional interests, and act only for the common good.

Emile (1762)

An essay on education, which argues for the possibility of a 'natural' education, free of the corruptions of modern society, whereby people might be reared to be cooperative and respectful their fellows.

The Confessions (1782)

Extraordinary autobiography, characterized by its honesty, which charts the course of Rousseau's life from childhood to old age.

govern their affairs given present circumstances? It was this question that Rousseau sought to answer in his most famous work, *The Social Contract*.

In contradistinction to the concerns of **Machiavelli**, for example, in writing this work, Rousseau was primarily interested in the normative question of the legitimacy of sovereign power. The argument he constructed rests on the concept of 'the general will'. Prior to living in social groups, individuals are free to pursue their own specific, selfish interests. However, once people begin to live in fixed relations with other people, this kind of freedom is necessarily curtailed. Nevertheless, there is a way in which people may live in social groups yet remain free; that is, if each individual member of the group forms part of that group's sovereign body. Freedom then consists in acting in accordance with the 'general will' of the group.

The 'General Will'

The idea of the 'general will' is more than a little slippery. It requires that individuals when acting as members of the sovereign body set aside their own personal, sectional interests and act only for the common good. Whether this is possible in practice is a moot point. Rousseau himself was clear that certain conditions would have be to met before it was even a possibility. Particularly, it requires the abolition of extreme wealth and poverty, and the existence of an educational system which would churn out citizens willing to act for the good of all. It also requires that the government, whatever form it takes (and Rousseau was not entirely prescriptive in this regard), separate and subordinate to the sovereign body, acts in line with the general will of the people.

Perhaps the major criticism which it is possible to level at the idea of the general will is that in effect it amounts to a dictatorship of the majority. This clearly was not Rousseau's intention; although he talked about people being 'forced to be free', he was nevertheless committed to the ends of liberty and freedom. However, the problem is a real one; not least because it just isn't obvious that there is any such thing as a 'common good' – it might just be that people have genuine but competing interests.

The Social Contract was published in 1762. This year marked something of a downturn in Rousseau's fortunes. Although he was at his intellectual peak, *Emile*, his treatise on education, attracted the attention of the authorities, and he was forced to flee Paris. Much of the writing of the remainder of his life constituted a defence of the positions he had set out in earlier work. He was also increasingly troubled by paranoia, becoming convinced that his old Enlightenment friends and sparring partners – Diderot, **Voltaire**, d'Alembert and the others – were plotting against him, and he even suspected that David **Hume**, who had helped him travel to England, was part of the conspiracy. However, despite his difficulties, he was in the latter period of his life able to start and complete, amongst other works, his great autobiography, *Confessions*, which even by today's standards is remarkable in its candour.

He died in 1778 with his reputation assured. His commitment to liberty and equality meant that he was soon to become an important symbol of the French Revolution. His ideas even today retain their importance; not only are his major works part of the standard canon of political theory, he also remains an influential figure in thinking about communitarian and socialist politics.

Once people begin to live in fixed relations with other people, freedom is necessarily curtailed.

Immanuel Kant

Ludwig Wittgenstein once remarked, and he may well have had Immanuel Kant (1724–1804) in mind, that reading philosophy is 'a kind of agony'. Kant's writing is spectacularly labyrinthine.

KANT'S FLAIR FOR INVENTING TECHNICAL VOCABULARY IS SOMETIMES LOST ON THOSE who notice the subtly different ways he uses those inventions, leaving the reader to keep track of the shifts with increasingly panic-stricken notes in the margins. His apparently morbid fear of punctuation results in sentences with lengths one never imagined possible – pages seem to float past as one loses all hope of a full stop. Despite all this, there is no question that Kant is among the very greatest of great philosophers.

Kant was born, lived and died in Königsberg, Prussia (now Kaliningrad, Russia). Except for a few, tentative, brief and short-ranging excursions, he never left. He studied at the local high school, attended the University of Königsberg, and eventually took a post as lecturer there, becoming Professor of Logic and Metaphysics in 1770.

Kant's rigid habits were legendary. A well-known story has it that the housewives of Königsberg set their clocks by his afternoon walks, which he took with awe-inspiring regularity, his servant trudging dutifully behind with an umbrella in case of rain. His dinner parties were organized around a careful timetable, with precisely regimented portions of the evening spent in political discussion, the telling of amusing anecdotes, music, and so on. Guests reported that the evenings at Kant's were excellent affairs, with one accomplishing all one could hope to achieve in a single evening. Having become accustomed to the life-long habit of breakfasting alone, he asked an unannounced friend to leave the table one morning, finding himself incapable of getting through the toast and tea in company.

It is not clear how much these stories should be believed, particularly as we do have the testimonies of many of his students, which do not quite agree with the stern caricatures above. The following is representative:

> In his prime he had the happy sprightliness of a youth; he continued to have it, I believe, even as a very old man. His broad forehead, built for thinking, was the seat of an imperturbable cheerfulness and joy. Speech, the richest in thought, flowed from his lips. Playfulness, wit and humour were at his command. His lectures were the most entertaining talks.

Although Kant himself was not geographically wide-ranging, his lectures, early writings and interests certainly were. He wrote and lectured on geography, mathematics, anthropology, physics, cosmology and biology, as well as logic, metaphysics and ethics. He continued his lectures, but did not publish anything for a period of nearly ten years. This was because Kant was quietly developing an entirely new approach to the fundamental questions of philosophy.

The Critiques

He broke the silence in 1781 with the publication of a masterpiece, *The Critique of Pure Reason*. Within a decade, this work was followed by two more of equal or nearly equal standing, *The Critique of Practical Reason* and *The Critique of Judgement*. And in the decade before his death in 1804, he published a number of other important books. The three Critiques contain nothing less than Kant's solutions to the main problems of metaphysics, ethics and aesthetics. We will have a look at at his ideas.

Kant notes that metaphysics has always seemed at war with itself. Arguments of apparently equal force might be levelled for and against the claims that the world has a beginning in time and is spatially limited, that every composite substance consists of simple substances, that free will exists, and that there is a God. Progress seems beyond us. We are compelled to wonder about these sorts of things, but when we bring reason to bear on them, we flounder in contradiction – or worse, despair in scepticism. Kant writes: 'Human reason has this peculiar fate that in one species of its knowledge it is burdened by questions which, as prescribed by the very nature of reason itself, it is not able to ignore, but which, as transcending all its powers, it is also not able to answer.'

This is particularly perplexing, as our rational capacities otherwise are essential to getting about the business of life. Kant proposes a critique or self-examination of reason, to determine its limits and proper employment. The hope is to end the otherwise interminable contradictions in metaphysics, as well as to provide some assurance that reason is a trustworthy guide when operating in its proper domain. Kant, then, calls upon:

> reason to undertake anew the most difficult of all its tasks, namely, that of self-knowledge, and to institute a tribunal which will assure to reason its lawful claims, and dismiss all groundless pretensions, not by despotic decrees, but in accordance with its own eternal and unalterable laws. This tribunal is no other than the *critique of pure reason*.

The Nature of Experience

Perhaps the best-known result of this critique is Kant's remarkable view on the role of the subject with respect to the nature of the experienced world. Before Kant, the mind was regarded as a passive recorder of the passing show. The metaphors for this view are familiar: the mind is the mirror of nature, like a blank slate upon which experience writes, like a lump of wax awaiting the impression of nature's signet ring. If the mind manages to conform to the way the world really is, the subject is said to know something about the world. Kant turns this conception upside-down. In what he called a revolution of Copernican proportions, Kant maintains that the mind is

The question of free will remains an open one in Kant's philosophy.

active, playing a part in shaping the world of experience. Instead of knowledge consisting in our minds conforming to a world of objects, Kant maintains that objects must conform to our minds.

This is much more than a mere reworking of **Locke**'s claim that some properties are mind-dependent – such things as colour and smell are not in the objects themselves, but depend upon a relation of subject and object. Rather, Kant holds that the mind categorizes and organizes all that is received in sensory experience in the forms of space and time and further shapes this input with such categories as cause and substance. The mind plays a part in the nature of the whole empirical world.

How does this revolution solve the problems of metaphysics? Since objects must conform to the powers of the mind in order to appear to us as objects in the first place, our knowledge of objects is knowledge of appearances. The very notion of an appearance presupposes something more, namely, a reality beyond appearances. Kant makes a distinction, then, between appearances (phenomena) and things-in-themselves (noumena), things as they are apart from experience. We can know something about appearances, but we can only think about things-in-themselves, and this is why metaphysics leads to contradictions. Metaphysical enquiry is an attempt to know things-in-themselves in terms of categories proper only to the world as we experience it.

Because causation is the result of our mind's categorizing activities, reason rightly looks for causes when events are perceived – a world of objects in space and time is unthinkable without causation. However, when we attempt to apply the concept to the universe as a whole, as it is in itself, and wonder whether or not the universe itself is caused, we have wandered beyond reason's proper domain, and contradictions are unavoidable.

This line of thinking shows why all speculative metaphysics is suspect, but it makes knowledge of the empirical world possible, and assures reason a secure role in our understanding of the phenomenal world. While Kant undercuts metaphysics, he nevertheless leaves room for certain truths. Think again about causation. If it is not possible to think of the world as we experience it without the concept of causality, then for the empirical world, every event has a cause. There is no appearance of human freedom. This view leaves open the question of whether or not human beings, considered as things-in-themselves, really are free. With the question of free will open, there is room for morality.

Doing the Right Thing

Kant's conception of morality is firmly rooted in reason, and it is a departure from other accounts which claim that morality must be based on sentiment or even the consequences of action. For Kant, doing the right thing is not a matter of one's character or disposition or circumstance – all of which are or might be beyond one's control. Instead, it is a matter of duty, acting out of respect for the moral law. The moral law, Kant argues, cannot be hypothetical in nature, cannot be of the form, 'If you want such and such, do so and so.' Wants and consequences cannot figure into what is morally right. Instead, the law itself must be categorical, of the form, 'Do this' or 'Don't do that.' Kant offers the following formulation of the so-called 'categorical imperative': 'Act only on that maxim whereby you can at the same time will that it should become a universal law.'

An example, Kant's own, might make all of this more clear. Suppose the rent is due, and you are in serious financial difficulty; your troubles are likely to be unending for the foreseeable future. You approach a friend for a loan, and she agrees, with the proviso that you promise to repay it by next week. You know this is impossible, but you contemplate making the false promise anyway, knowing there is no chance of repaying the loan.

Kant argues that actions are undertaken under maxims or rules, and the rule you are contemplating is this: 'When I think I need some money, I will borrow it and promise to repay it, though I know I never can do so.' Kant's test for such maxims is universalizability: suppose the maxim you are considering were to become a universal law, a maxim adopted by everybody. Would the system thus engendered be consistent or self-contradictory? If the former, you are in no danger of doing the wrong thing, but if the latter, you are in violation of the moral law. If everybody made false promises, promising itself would be impossible – who would believe a promise? The maxim you were contemplating results in a self-contradiction, and it is therefore not in keeping with the categorical imperative. Don't do it.

The morality pie can be cut in lots of ways, but a large slice is reserved for the Kantians, and arguments between duty-based ethicists and consequentialists show no sign of slowing down. It is probably not possible to understand much in contemporary ethics without knowing at least the bare outlines of Kant's thinking. It is certainly impossible to understand German philosophy since Kant without knowing a great deal about Kant himself. His view of the human mind as somehow actively constituting the empirical world, radical in his day, is now an obvious presupposition in many quarters. Although Kant himself did not travel, it is clear that his thinking is now everywhere in philosophy.

MAJOR WORKS

Critique of Pure Reason (1781)

Kant's masterpiece and one of the most unique and philosophically impressive books ever written. Its most astonishing insight is the claim that the mind plays an active role in constituting the objects of knowledge.

Critique of Practical Reason (1788)

Contains Kant's formulation of the moral law and an in-depth discussion of the relation between the ideas God, human freedom, immortality and the very notion of morality.

Critique of Judgement (1790)

Kant's consideration of aesthetics, in particular the judgements we make about the nature of the beautiful and the sublime.

Thomas Paine

Thomas Paine (1737–1809) would play a part in bringing about the American revolution with his political essays and pamphlets; however, his later work would lose him friends in America.

THOMAS PAINE WAS BORN IN THETFORD, ENGLAND, on 29 January, 1737. For the next 37 years, he lived a life of impressive mediocrity. He failed in a variety of professions, including teaching, tobacco selling and tax collection. His marriage was something of a disaster, with some biographers reporting that even before formally separating from his wife in 1774, Paine had never lived together with her. And when, aged 17, he had attempted to run away to sea, he was captured on board ship by his father, who carried him back home again.

Paine's early lack of success was not entirely surprising. Unlike many of the great philosophers, he had not been born into privilege. His father Joseph Paine, a Quaker, was a corset maker by profession. This did not bring in much money. Indeed, Thomas Paine recounted later that it had cost his parents some hardship to send him to the local grammar school: 'My parents were not able to give me a shilling, beyond what they gave me in education; and to do this they distressed themselves.'

One of the strongest natural proofs of the folly of hereditary right in kings, is, that nature disapproves it.

However, though Paine's early years were inauspicious, there were aspects of his upbringing which left an indelible stamp on his character, and which informed the political writings that were later to make him famous. In particular, the Quakerism of his father gave him the strong sense that all human beings are born fundamentally equal and the moral courage required to pursue a reforming agenda.

The transformation in his fortunes, when it came, happened very quickly. In October 1774, on the recommendation of Benjamin Franklin, whom he had met when seeking to interest parliament in a tax relief measure, he had sailed for America. He carried a letter of introduction written by Franklin, and on the strength of it he was able to secure a job, first as a writer for *Pennsylvania Magazine*, and then as its editor. It was here that he wrote his first notable article; a call for the abolition of slavery, which he signed off 'Justice and Humanity'.

Common Sense

He followed this up with the essay which was to make him famous. 'Common Sense' was published early in 1776, and it had an immediate impact. In it, Paine

Satirical cartoon by Gillray, depicting Thomas Paine's Nightly Pest, *an unpleasant vision of what would await him should he ever return to Britain.*

argued that it was both a moral duty and practical necessity for America to seek independence from Great Britain. He attacked the idea of a hereditary monarchy, partly on the grounds that it violated a principle of equality which is rooted in the natural condition of humankind:

> For all men being originally equal, no one by birth could have a right to set up his own family in perpetual preference to all others for ever, and though himself might deserve some decent degree of honour of his contemporaries, yet his descendants might be far too unworthy to inherit them. One of the strongest natural proofs of the folly of hereditary right in kings, is, that nature disapproves it, otherwise she would not so frequently turn it into ridicule by giving mankind an ass for a lion.

For Paine, it was unthinkable that America should continue to be ruled by a British king. He argued that such an eventuality would result in North America being kept as low as possible by their master. He also claimed that American independence, and the establishment of a republican form of government, founded on the principle of the equality of its citizens, was the best way of avoiding the possibility of civil conflict.

There is no doubting the influence of 'Common Sense'. It not only persuaded many of the major figures in the American Revolution of the merits of an independent America, but it also sold in large numbers – 120,000 in the first three months after publication – to the general populace. Paine continued his writing to great effect throughout the War of Independence. Indeed, shortly before the battle of Trenton, George Washington had called his demoralized soldiers together in groups so that Paine could be read aloud to them in order to improve their morale:

> These are the times that try men's souls. The summer soldier and the sunshine patriot will, in this crisis, shrink from the service of his country; but he that stands it now, deserves the love and thanks of man and woman. Tyranny, like hell, is not easily conquered; yet we have this consolation with us, that the harder the conflict the more glorious the triumph: what we obtain too cheap we esteem too lightly; it is dearness only that gives everything its value.

Thomas Paine

The Rights of Man

After the war, Paine briefly held a couple of government jobs, before returning to England where he wrote what is perhaps his most important work, *The Rights of Man*. It was a primarily a defence of the principles of the French Revolution against the criticisms which Edmund Burke had levelled against it in his *Reflections*. Developing a theme which had first appeared in 'Common Sense', Paine argued that people are born with equal, natural rights. However, they do not live as isolated individuals, but rather in societies where they enjoy the benefits of cooperation and sociality. Unfortunately, in such circumstances, it is almost inevitable that from time to time the rights of people will be violated, because human beings are far from perfect. Consequently, in order to secure all natural rights, people will deposit those rights which they cannot uphold individually – for example, the right to redress for a harm – into the protection of government.

According to Paine, this means that government is only legitimate when it is established by the people as a whole; that is, government must be of the people, and for the people. This rules out hereditary monarchy straight away, because this form of government involves a previous generation determining the rulers of future generations. In fact, it was Paine's contention that the only legitimate form of government is democratic republicanism; it best represents the aggregate rights which people are unable to defend individually, and which they therefore give up to government in order that all rights are secured.

Perhaps more radically, Paine also used *The Rights of Man* to outline in some detail a system of welfare, with the aim of addressing the social deprivation associated with poverty. He noted that the gallows seemed to be the exclusive province of the poor, and argued that this was a sign of government gone wrong:

> Why is it, that scarcely any are executed but the poor? The fact is a proof, among other things, of a wretchedness in their condition. Bred up without morals, and cast upon the world without a prospect, they are the exposed sacrifice of vice and legal barbarity. The millions that are superfluously wasted upon governments, are more than sufficient to reform those evils, and to benefit the condition of every man in a nation, not included within the purlieus of a court.

All this proved too much for the British establishment. In May 1792, a royal proclamation was issued against seditious writing, and Paine was charged with treason, causing him to flee to France, never to return. At first, he was welcomed in France, even gaining a seat at the National Convention. However, things soon became difficult for Paine. He was denounced by the Jacobin leader Robespierre for his association with the Girondins, a moderate republican group, and was arrested very soon after completing his book *The Age of Reason*, in which he argued for deism against both atheism and Christianity.

Paine very nearly lost his life in the Jacobin Terror, but was eventually freed when the American statesman James Monroe intervened on his behalf. After his release from prison, Paine carried on writing. In *Agrarian Justice*, published in 1797, he returned to questions of social justice and basic rights. He argued that the mark of a civilized state *ought* to be that it leaves no individual worse off than they would have been had they been born before civilization existed. However, he noted that in fact the poor in every country in Europe were worse off than the native American Indians of North America. He put this down to the fact that more than half the inhabitants of every nation had been dispossessed of landed property.

The proper response to this situation is not collective ownership, as was suggested by Karl **Marx** more than 100 years later, but rather a system of land and property tax, with the proceeds going into a National Fund and then being redistributed amongst all the people of a nation. Paine emphasized that this was not a matter of charity, but of rights. As inhabitants of Earth, every person has an equal claim over Earth in its natural state. The proposed National Fund would compensate for the fact that most people – for sensible reasons – were unable to succeed in this claim.

Reason and Superstition

In 1802, Paine returned to America, the land where he had first made his name. However, he was much less popular on his return than he had been when he had left some 20 years earlier. His arguments in *The Age of Reason*, particularly his attacks on the vengeful and spiteful God of the Bible, had alienated many in the New World. Consequently, though he continued writing until his death, Paine lived out the remaining years of his life in ill-health and obscurity.

There is a parallel here with how Paine has been treated by history. Although his writings were hugely influential during his lifetime, and he has remained something of a hero to people on the British Left, he is not normally considered to be in the top rank of philosophers. This is partly because his work lacks the sophistication and learning of people like John **Locke** and Karl Marx. However, to criticize Paine for this reason would be to misunderstand the intent of his writing. He was addressing a popular audience. He had the ability – which all too many philosophers lack – to write in a clear prose style; of affecting people, and getting them to see their traditional attitudes and values in a new light. To read Paine even today is still to be struck by the power and integrity of his voice.

MAJOR WORKS

'Common Sense' (1776)

The essay which made Thomas Paine famous. Exploding on to the scene in the middle of the War of Independence, it argues for the independence of America from Great Britain, both on moral and practical grounds.

The Rights of Man (1792)

A defence of the principles of the French revolution against the criticisms set out in Edmund Burke's *Reflections on the French Revolution*. Its central thesis is that the only legitimate form of government – of the people, and for the people – was democratic republicanism.

The Age of Reason (1794)

This work outlines the case for an enlightened deism, but perhaps more significantly includes an assault on the vengeful God of the Christian Bible, which alienated many of Paine's supporters in the New World.

Agrarian Justice (1797)

This book argues for a system of land and property tax, with the proceeds going into a National Fund, and then being redistributed amongst all the people of a nation. Paine emphasises that this was not a matter of charity, but of rights.

Jeremy Bentham

Jeremy Bentham (1748–1832) was perhaps as much a social reformer as a philosopher, and is also well-known for his many inventions. His major contribution to philosophy is the theory of utilitarianism.

1748–1832

IF YOU ARE FEELING A LITTLE GHOULISH AND FIND YOURSELF AT A LOOSE END and in London, you can do worse than wander into the cloisters of University College. You will discover, encased in a mahogany and glass structure, nothing less than the mortal remains of Jeremy Bentham seated in his usual chair in an attitude of relaxed contemplation and dressed in suitably restrained clothing, his favourite cane propped by his side. If you are very ghoulish you might be saddened to learn that the head is a wax dummy, though the skeleton under the clothes is real enough. The actual head, preserved 'in the manner of the New Zealanders', remains in the university's safe for two reasons: first, the preservation process was not entirely successful, and it is probably too ghastly for display; second, it has gone missing a number of times. The pious students of King's College, natural enemies of the humanists of University College, have absconded with it on at least two occasions – it was once discovered in a luggage locker in the Aberdeen rail station.

The auto-icon, as it is called, was entirely Bentham's idea, and his reasons for it are outlined in his last work, *Auto-Icon; Or, Farther Uses of the Dead to the Living*. Much of the book has to be tongue-in-cheek – it includes Bentham's suggestion that the preserved bodies of the famous might serve as excellent lawn ornaments. But the auto-icon has a practical aim: the inspiration in his followers of certain useful feelings and beliefs. Bentham, though born to a line of lawyers and himself called to the bar in 1767, busied himself throughout his life not in the courtroom, but with all manner of practical schemes.

A Practical Mind

He worked on projects involving portable houses; a canal in Central America; a new prison design, the infamous Panopticon, which he hoped would 'grind rogues honest'; central heating systems; refrigeration units; and counterfeit-proof bank notes. He had 'conversation tubes' installed in his London home and slept in a sleeping bag of his own devising. He also coined a remarkable number of words: 'maximize', 'minimize', 'rationale', 'demoralize', 'dynamic', 'unilateral', 'detachable', 'exhaustive', 'cross-examination', 'international' and 'codification' among them. Not all of Bentham's neologisms gained currency. Sadly, we have all but lost 'catastaticochrestic physiurgics'.

It is clear that John Stuart **Mill** was right to say that Bentham had an 'essentially practical mind'. The projects he undertook throughout his life, even that of finding a use for himself after death, were all aimed at solving problems Bentham himself had identified. The problems which most exercised him, though, were difficulties in the law. His proposed solutions led to a political movement in which the variously named Benthamites, Utilitarians or Philosophical Radicals agitated for social and legal reform in line with Bentham's own thinking. Bentham and his followers proposed enlightened changes to the law on the treatment of animals, property, taxation, homosexuality, poverty, suffrage and much else. A large number of these proposals actually became law under the Reform Bill of 1832, and it is a clear fact that many lives have been the better for it.

Bentham saw, from a young age, inconsistencies in the very foundations of social and legal practices. As a student at Westminster School, Bentham was required to sign the Articles of Religion of the Church of England, but he identified in them numerous falsehoods, as well as contradictions with the actual teachings of the Church. At Oxford University, he was a student of the legal scholar William Blackstone, but found himself unable to follow the lectures, fretted as they were with fallacious thinking. The difficulty, as Bentham saw it, lies in a kind of irrationality at the heart of the law. The law and the punishments it metes out seem tied not to rational principle, but to fictions, falsehoods and whatever it is which happens to offend the lawmakers most.

Instead of the arbitrary intuitions of lawmakers, Bentham grounds legal decision-making on a psychological fact: people act in their own interests, and those interests consist of getting pleasure and avoiding pain. Individual human happiness, then, consists in achieving a greater balance of pleasure over pain for the greatest number of people. We have here the beginnings of a system of value and a conception of the moral good rooted in human nature. Thus Bentham identifies a principle that is both moral and legal, the Principle of Utility or the Greatest Happiness Principle. He characterizes it as follows:

> By the principle of utility is meant that principle which approves or disapproves of every action whatsoever, according to the tendency which it appears to have to augment or diminish the happiness of the party whose interest is in question ... I say that of every action whatsoever; and therefore not only of every action of a private individual, but of every measure of government.

The view, then, is obviously consequentialist. What makes an action right or wrong are its effects, in particular, its psychological effects on people.

There is an immediate difficulty with this proposal: it presupposes something apparently ridiculous, that pleasure is somehow quantifiable. There are, happily, many pleasures. Clearly, some pleasures are more pleasurable than others, but is it possible to say just how much more pleasurable? If I adopt

MAJOR WORKS

A Fragment on Government (1776)
An attack on the notion of tradition in law, as opposed to the grounding of law in rational principle. It contains much else, in particular arguments against certain dubious conceptions of political obligation.

Introduction to the Principles of Morals and Legislation (1789)
Provides an outline of the basis of Bentham's proposed rational reform of law and morality. It includes a detailed account of the greatest happiness principle.

Bentham's principle, I must choose those actions which issue in a greater balance of pleasure over pain, but this can only be done if I have a clear way of comparing pleasures with pleasures, pains with pains, and pleasures with pains.

I happen to be free tonight – what to do? Shall I indulge my lust for sushi, go to the cinema, help the homeless, read some Walt Whitman, have a nap, repair to the pub? Is the pub a bit more pleasurable than eating sushi but less pleasurable than a nap or not quite as pleasurable as reading? Would the help I offer the homeless result in their pleasure, which is, in itself, greater than the pleasure I might take in a nap? Would helping the homeless bring them some pleasure which is immediately cancelled by the pain of my regret at being unable to do enough? I have no way of ranking or quantifying this morass of possible pleasure and pain, as it seems Bentham requires.

The Arithmetic of Pleasure

Bentham's solution, the hedonistic calculus, is precisely what one expects from a resolutely practical mind – he not only claims that pleasure is quantifiable but offers a system for its quantification. He identifies several factors which might figure into any such calculation: the pleasure's intensity, duration, certainty, propinquity, fecundity, purity and extent. Further, he considers the relative merits of kinds of pleasure (the pleasure attending sensation, possession, skill, friendship, reputation, power and malevolence) as well as the demerits of different kinds of pain (the pain of want, disappointment, regret, and so on). More than this, Bentham admits that pleasure

Bentham's Panopticon prison, where the prisoners can be observed at any time by the warder; this, believed Bentham, would lead to the prisoners developing the habit of good behaviour.

and pain are, in some sense, relative to the perceiver, and this relativity itself depends on such factors as a person's education, religion, and social standing – all of this must be taken into account. So, in choosing a course of action, we must: 'Sum up all the values of all the pleasures on the one side, and those of all the pains on the other. The balance, if it be on the side of pleasure, will give the good tendency of the act up on the whole.'

Our lawmakers, then, have much to consider in formulating our laws. Enforcing the law, too, can become a little complicated. Suppose a string of heinous crimes is committed in a community. The crimes themselves cause pain to the victims, certainly, but there is further pain in the form of insecurity and anxiety suffered by everyone who fears they might be next. Perhaps there is a lot of suffering; worry that the government has lost control of the streets; maybe something near panic is in danger of breaking out. Think of the pain such fear might cause.

A good utilitarian law enforcement agent might reason as follows. We are holding someone from out of town for a minor traffic offence, someone with no known connection to these heinous crimes. Might it relieve the anxiety of the community, and improve the overall balance of pleasure over pain considerably, if we make this person a scapegoat? We could plant some evidence on him, charge him with the crimes, publicly punish him, maybe even execute him (by painless lethal injection, if you like). Maybe this will deter the real criminal. It would certainly reduce anxiety. Is this sort of thing not only permitted by the Greatest Happiness Principle, but required by it? In this example at least – and one is enough – are we not morally compelled to kill someone we know is innocent?

The Problem of Justice

This might be called 'the problem of justice' for Bentham. It seems, in the above case anyway, that certain things follow from the utilitarian view which conflict with our intuitions about what is just or at least what is right. The counter-example can tug in two directions. It can be concluded from it that utilitarianism cannot be the right way to think about morality, or it can be concluded that intuitions about justice are wrong.

The problem itself might be cast more generally: sometimes the only way to bring about a greater balance of pleasure over pain is by one or more of us suffering for someone else. Obviously, this is not to claim that the poor ought to suffer for the sake of the rich, quite the reverse. It is to get near a truth about the connection between putting aside one's desires for someone else's and the nature of morality. Utilitarianism captures something about what many take to be a fact about any moral system worth the name: its impersonal nature. Morality requires your interests sometimes standing in for my own –and this is the important bit – no matter who you are. Perhaps Bentham's view captures this starkly, and our quibble with it reflects not a fault in utilitarianism, but the fact that being moral is not easy.

If you do make the pilgrimage and inspect Bentham's bones, take a moment to stand back a little and observe the students slouching past on their way to the library. If you watch carefully enough and long enough, you will notice a few passers-by staring at Bentham, perhaps nodding almost imperceptibly, unconsciously. These are invariably philosophy students at University College, who know something of our debt to Bentham.

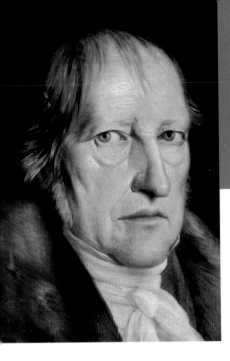

Georg Hegel

Georg Hegel (1770–1831) occupies a rather strange position in the history of philosophical thought: he is both extremely influential and almost impossible for a non-specialist to understand.

1770–1831

TWO OF HEGEL'S MOST IMPORTANT WORKS, *The Phenomenology of Spirit* and *The Science of Logic* contain some of the most difficult philosophical writing which has yet appeared. Indeed, the impenetrability of his prose has led some people to suspect that he was a charlatan; that he deliberately obfuscated in order to create the appearance of profundity where, in fact, none existed.

However, this is to be uncharitable; Hegel's is a systematic philosophy – indeed, he is arguably the last great system builder in philosophy – and at least some of the difficulty of his work is linked to the magnitude of the task he set himself. His aim was nothing less than to develop the conceptual apparatus necessary to understand the whole of reality, or, as he called it, Absolute Spirit. But even so, close reading of his work will eventually bear fruit; certainly it is possible for readers without a background in philosophy to get something from texts like *Lectures on the History of Philosophy* and *The Philosophy of Right*.

Hegel was born on 27 August 1770 in Stuttgart. As the son of an official in the government of the Duke of Württemberg, he enjoyed a comfortable, middle-class upbringing. He was educated at the local grammar school, and although he did not show the precocious abilities of a **Pascal** or a **Peirce**, he was nevertheless a first-class student. His taste for systematic and methodical work was evident even in these early years: for example, as a schoolboy, he kept a diary in which he carefully charted the progress of his reading; and at the age of 16, he started an alphabetized collection of the detailed notes he took from the books he read.

Hegel's dialectical method is best understood in terms of the concepts of thesis, antithesis, and synthesis.

His father wanted him to become a clergyman, so in 1788, Hegel entered the Protestant seminary at Tübingen. Although he successfully completed his studies there, his teachers reported that whilst he had excelled in philosophy, he had not appeared particularly interested in theology. Not surprisingly, then, he decided against a career in the church, and instead pursued his ambition to attain an academic position; this he achieved, with the help of his friend Schelling, when he took up a post at the University of Jena in 1801.

It was while he was at Jena that Hegel put together *The Phenomenology of Spirit*, probably his most famous work. In it, he attempted to show, roughly speaking, how consciousness develops via a dialectical process, until it recognizes that it is identical with the whole of reality, which itself is pure thought or spirit. Unfortunately, this idea is every bit as complex as it sounds. Perhaps the most fruitful way to gain a sense of it is to consider what is involved in the idea of dialectical progress.

The Dialectical Method

Hegel's dialectical method is best understood in terms of the concepts of thesis, antithesis, and synthesis. Put simply, the idea is that any given phenomenon (thesis) contains within itself contradictory aspects (antithesis) which require a movement towards resolution (synthesis); and that progress in our understanding of reality occurs according to an iterative process which has this dialectical form. It is possible to illustrate this idea by looking at how Hegel thought that an individual self-consciousness moves towards self-certainty.

The idea of self-certainty is a complex one; however, it seems to be most clearly expressed by the notion of 'belongingness'. Hegel had in mind that self-consciousness aims towards a situation where there is nothing in external reality which is alien to it; where, in a strong sense, self-consciousness is synonymous with the reality which it constitutes. Part of the significance of this journey to self-certainty is that it underpins the original relationship between self-consciousness and things which are other to it.

In Hegel's scheme, self-consciousness emerges when consciousness recognizes the reflection of itself in the objects towards which it is directed. Thus, 'consciousness of another, of an object in general, is in fact necessarily self-consciousness, reflectedness in self, consciousness of oneself in one's other'. However, whilst self-consciousness requires an external object to define itself, it is at the same time threatened by this object. The external object is foreign to the self; it is an otherness, in the face of which self-consciousness is unable to attain self-certainty. Thus,

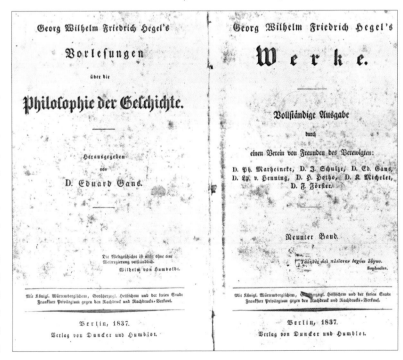

Title page of Hegel's Philosophy of History. *This is one of the most accessible of Hegel's works, despite its 480-page length.*

in a state of *desire*, self-consciousness seeks to negate the otherness of the external object by assimilating it. In the words of Hegel 'self-consciousness presents itself here as the process in which this opposition is removed, and oneness or identity with itself established'.

However, with the negation of the otherness of the external object comes a difficulty: if this entails the object's destruction, then self-consciousness, dependent upon the moment of otherness, is robbed of the foundations of its own existence.

Therefore, self-consciousness requires an object which can be negated, whose foreignness can be annulled, without the object itself being destroyed. According to Hegel, only another self-consciousness fulfils this requirement, since only this is able to effect its own negation, and yet remain an external object. Specifically, he claims that a self-consciousness must seek the acknowledgement and recognition of other self-conscious beings; only in this way can it attain the self-certainty it desires.

Master and Slave

With this insight, therefore, that 'self consciousness exists in itself and for itself, in that, and by the fact that it exists for another self-consciousness', we are led to the famous dialectic of master and slave. Although mutual recognition between self-consciousnesses will ultimately bring the self-certainty that these seek, this will not be easily won. At first, neither self-consciousness is certain of the truth of the other – as self-consciousness – and hence both are deprived of the source of their own certainty. Consequently, each will try to attain the recognition of the other without reciprocating.

According to Hegel, the resulting struggle – for one-sided recognition – is necessarily to the death, because, in risking their own lives, these self-consciousnesses can demonstrate to each other, and to themselves, their freedom from their particular bodily forms, and hence their status as *beings for themselves*. However, it is clear that in this context the death of either participant would be irrelevant, since it would completely deprive the survivor of recognition. Hence, the solution to the struggle for one-sided recognition, which must put the life of each participant in danger, is the enslavement of one and the mastery of the other: 'The one is independent, and its essential nature is to be for itself; the other is dependent, and its essence is life or existence for another. The former is the Master, or Lord, the latter the Bondsman' (*The Phenomenology of Spirit*).

However, it is Hegel's view that the opposition between individuals is something which will in time be overcome. The dialectic of master and slave, and the conflict which this entails, is simply one of the phases which self-consciousness must pass through on its way to self-certainty. Interestingly, it is the slave, and not

MAJOR WORKS

Phenomenology of Spirit (1807)

Hegel's most celebrated work. Employing his characteristic dialectical methodology, it tracks the unfolding of Being, or Absolute Spirit, across the whole of history. It is an extraordinarily difficult book, but also hugely influential, setting in motion a whole tradition of philosophy in the nineteenth century.

The Science of Logic (1812–1816)

It sets down, systematically and in detail, the basis of Hegel's metaphysical logic. The dialectical method is employed in order to articulate the abstract categories of thought, with the conclusion in the end being that reality is constituted by the Absolute.

Elements of the Philosophy of Right (1821)

The most mature statement of Hegel's social and political philosophy. In it, Hegel suggested that the most rational state was similar to the existing Prussian monarchy. For this he was accused of selling out, and it led the Young Hegelians to develop their own version of Hegelianism, one which in their eyes was nearer to the spirit of the real Hegel.

Lectures on the Philosophy of History (1833–1836)

One of the easiest entries into Hegel's ideas, compiled from lecture notes after his death, it tracks the progress of freedom across time and in the context of different kinds of society.

the master, who takes the next steps on the journey; transformed by the experience of work, the slave comes to possess the intellectual tools necessary to progress to a greater self-understanding.

The Philosophy of History

Hegel employed a similar dialectical method in order to analyse the unfolding of human history. In his view, human history is characterized by the move towards greater freedom, rationality and understanding. As he put it in the introduction to *Lectures on the Philosophy of History*, 'The history of the world is none other than the progress of the consciousness of freedom.'

In this book, which was compiled from lecture notes after his death, he tracked this progress of freedom through the examples of various kinds of society. Thus, in ancient oriental regimes, such as China, only the despot is free; the people who make up the populace of these societies lack even the knowledge that they have the ability to make autonomous judgements. Although Hegel thought that the citizens of the city-states of ancient Greece enjoyed a certain truncated freedom, he said that it was only with the Reformation that the idea of individual freedom found proper expression. History from this point on can be understood as the series of changes which societies underwent in order to get to grips with this new concept of freedom. Thus, the Enlightenment, though it led to the excesses of Jacobin terror, and demonstrated that there could be no absolute break with the past, was nevertheless an attempt to reconstruct modern societies in terms of the precepts of abstract universalism.

In Hegel's view, once an awareness of freedom has come to exist, it will eventually triumph; and in an echo of **Rousseau**, he said that politics then is about building communities which enable individuals to live out a freedom that is based upon their common ability to reason.

Hegel's ideas have had enormous impact on social and political thought over the last two hundred years. Most famously, **Marx** employed Hegel's dialectical method in the development of his historical materialism; indeed, in the early part of his life, Marx, along with people like Bruno Bauer and Ludwig Feuerbach, considered himself to be a young Hegelian. **Sartre**'s existentialism was also heavily indebted to Hegel; particularly, his analysis of being-for-others is predicated on a development of the insights contained in the master and slave section of *The Phenomenology of Spirit*.

However, it is also true that the kind of philosophy which Hegel represents, namely, the tradition which is fond of grand metaphysical speculation, has fallen on hard times. In particular, the rise of logical positivism in the twentieth century, with its claim that statements are meaningful only if they are true by definition or empirically verifiable, undermined the appeal of a philosophy like Hegel's. A. J. **Ayer**, for example, in his *Language, Truth and Logic*, had no difficulty in showing that Francis Bradley's Hegelian inspired version of idealism was constructed out of claims which were not in any obvious way meaningful. Indeed, for many people working in the analytic tradition of philosophy, Hegel's kind of philosophy is precisely what has to be avoided in order to produce good work. Therefore, whatever one thinks about the merits of his philosophical system, it is almost certain that we won't see the like of Hegel again for quite some time.

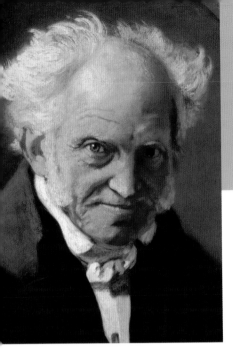

Arthur Schopenhauer

Although outside the realm of academic philosophy, Arthur Schopenhauer (1788–1860) was nevertheless one of the most important philosophers of the nineteenth century, best known for his Eastern influence, and his philosophical pessimism.

SCHOPENHAUER'S PHILOSOPHY IS STUNNINGLY AND FAMOUSLY PESSIMISTIC. His work is certainly not the right sort of thing to read on a beach. It is hard to know whether the pessimism is the result of his philosophical discoveries or, rather, his philosophy is shaped by his pessimism. It might be that both simply follow from his own generally bleak temperament. His mother, Johanna, reports that from an early age her son 'brooded on the misery of things'. Nevertheless, the broodings resulted in one of the nineteenth century's philosophical masterpieces: *The World as Will and Representation*. We'll consider it in a moment.

Schopenhauer was born in Danzig. His father, Heinrich, was a prosperous merchant, whose politics led him to move the family, at considerable cost, to Hamburg when Danzig was appropriated by Prussia in 1793. His parents encouraged his facility with languages – he was eventually fluent in six – and sent him to study in Paris and England. Although he would have preferred an academic life, he took a job as a clerk in Hamburg to satisfy his father. His father's suicide left Schopenhauer with no incentive to stay in business and a reasonable income, so he turned to an academic life. Taking a place at the University of Göttingen, Schopenhauer initially studied medicine but switched to philosophy. At the suggestion of his tutors he focused on **Plato** and **Kant**. These two philosophers, combined with the unlikely influence of Hinduism and Buddhism, had an enduring effect on his thinking. He submitted his dissertation to the University of Jena, earned a doctorate, and returned to his mother's home in Weimar.

His mother had an interest in culture, particularly literature, and published several novels. She also operated a literary salon and, quite possibly, had romantic liaisons with several representatives of Weimar's intelligentsia. This probably disturbed Schopenhauer. No doubt Schopenhauer's diatribes on the futility of existence, which led many guests of the salon to make excuses and leave a little early, disturbed his mother too. They fell out regularly, dramatically, and eventually comprehensively. Johanna demanded that he leave, and he departed for Dresden in 1814. Though his mother lived for another 24 years, they never spoke again.

Whether or not Schopenhauer would be willing to admit it, the episode skewed his thinking and probably had large effects on his per-

Schopenhauer is stunningly and famously pessimistic – not the right sort of material to read on a beach.

sonal life. You can hear the resentment when the otherwise clear-thinking Schopenhauer says that women are: '…an undersized, narrow-shouldered, broad-hipped and short-legged race … they have no proper knowledge of anything; and they have no genius.'

It almost goes without saying that despite a few romantic connections, Schopenhauer never married. He was the archetypal bachelor-philosopher, living and studying alone in Berlin and finally Frankfurt, with only his pet poodle for company. He died, seated at his breakfast table, in 1860.

The World as Will

The World as Will and Representation was published in 1818 and attracted virtually no interest. He attempted to drum up support by lecturing in Berlin, deliberately and disastrously timetabling his lectures to conflict with those of **Hegel**, whom he perhaps predictably regarded as 'a commonplace, inane, loathsome, repulsive and ignorant charlatan'. His lecture hall remained empty, and he never repeated the experiment. He did, however, believe in the intrinsic value of his work – he thought it solved all philosophical problems worth the name – and had a second, expanded edition published. It was not until late in his life that the book and other writings finally earned him the fame he was after.

The book, says Schopenhauer, imparts a single thought, though he admits he is incapable of saying it in anything less than a large volume. Let us be a little reck-

Pears on a chair. The experience of actual pears, says Schopenhauer, provokes the will; whereas an artistic representation of pears produces an aesthetic reaction.

less, and characterize this thought in a single sentence: the world as it is in itself is will. To get this single thought into clearer view, we'll need to wave briefly at **Kant**, to whom Schopenhauer owes a large debt.

Kant argues that the world we perceive is constituted by the mind. Objects appear to us in space and time, given the structuring activities of sensibility. Thanks to the understanding, we perceive a world of objects not just in space and time but standing in causal relations with one another as well. Schopenhauer follows Kant in all of this – although he ingeniously reduces Kant's complex structure of categories to a single principle. Crucially, he adopts the Kantian distinction between the phenomenal world we experience (the world as representation) and the noumenal world of things-in-themselves, reality as it is apart from our experience (for Schopenhauer, the world as will). However, he rejects Kant's claim that the noumenal world is forever beyond our ken. Schopenhauer claims nothing less than knowledge of the world as it is in itself.

Our sensory experience of the world is not our only access to the world, or at least not our only access to a part of the world. Schopenhauer argues that 'a way from *within* stands open to us to [the] real inner nature of things'. We have perceptual experience of ourselves as bodies located in a world of objects in space and time, but we also have direct experience of ourselves as will – experience which does not conform to the usual activities of the mind which constitute the phenomenal world. I know my hand just reached for the coffee cup because I saw it, but I would have known anyway, because I willed it. When I looked at my hand, I viewed it as an object in the phenomenal world, but my other knowledge of it depended on nothing phenomenal. It is important to recognize that, for Schopenhauer, the willing and the bodily moving are not two different things: my body is objectified will, will as it appears or is represented in the phenomenal world.

Resolutely shunning solipsism, here the view that there is just one mind and everything else is a mere appearance, Schopenhauer argues that the whole world is a manifestation of will too. Once a person has realized that their own inner nature is will,

> [h]e will recognize that same will not only in those phenomena that are quite similar to his own, in men and animals, as their innermost nature, but continued reflection will lead him to recognize the force that shoots and vegetates in the plant, indeed the force by which the crystal is formed, the force that turns the magnet...all these he will recognize as different only in the phenomenon, but the same according to their inner nature.

If you want to do better than agree with Schopenhauer on anti-solipsistic grounds, you can think along the following lines. If the will is the real inner nature of my body, and my body is lodged seamlessly into the rest of the phenomenal world, then the rest of the world's real inner nature must also be will. For Schopenhauer, the phenomenal world is the appearance of will and the noumenal world is nothing but a world of will. Our own inner experience of willing, then, is Schopenhauer's key to understanding the Kantian thing-in-itself, the world as it is apart from our experience.

The Philosophy of Pessimism

Considered in the abstract, the will is a kind of will-to-live or will-to-exist, but it manifests itself particularly as a constant throbbing of desire, striving and yearning, with no particular goal or object. It is merely undirected, blind, irrational want, which drives everything – better, which is everything. It is the blindness and irrationality of the will which leads to Schopenhauer's famous pessimism. A human life is actuated by nothing but a constant craving, occasionally fleetingly satisfied but more often than not thwarted. When the will actually manages to satisfy itself, 'life-benumbing boredom' quickly sets in and the striving is reawakened. The will does nothing but vainly keep itself willing, until death. Life is something which ought not to be, and this is the very worst of all possible worlds. The uselessness of life emerges rather readily on Schopenhauer's view of the inner nature of things:

> …existence…is a constant hurrying of the present into the dead past, a constant dying…it is clear that, as our walking is admittedly merely a constantly prevented falling, the life of our body is only a constantly prevented dying, an ever postponed death: finally, in the same way, the activity of our mind is a constantly deferred ennui. Every breath we draw wards off the death that is constantly intruding upon us.

You would consider throwing him out of the salon too.

All is not entirely lost. Schopenhauer argues that there is a sense in which the will, if not tamed or fully sated, can be distracted from its cravings through aesthetic contemplation. If not exactly a kind of transcendence, there is a marked difference between our reactions to seeing a bowl of fruit, on the one hand, and admiring a well-executed still life depicting a bowl of fruit on the other. In the first case, the will might well become aroused, perhaps wanting to consume the fruit; but in the second, no such involvement is possible. Instead, one is led to something akin to reflection on **Plato**'s Forms, something approaching disinterested will-less contemplation, reflection for its own sake.

However, this sort of escape is only fleeting – one cannot stare at paintings forever. Our best hope for a lasting, though imperfect, release from the tyranny of the will is the saintly renunciation of life. It is possible, though a rarity, to become fully cognizant of the genuine nature of things. One can grasp the essential futility of all life, see life for what it is: the blind cravings of a single, unified Cosmic Will. The ascetic reaction, the renunciation of all gratification, the turning away from life, is the only genuine way one might deny the will and thereby diminish it, perhaps nearly extinguish it. The Buddhists have got it right or nearly right, according to Schopenhauer. The ultimate state is nothing like a heaven of pure satisfaction and eternal happiness, but the nothingness of Nirvana. For Schopenhauer, then, the closest to happiness we can come consists in the extinction of the self.

MAJOR WORKS

On the Fourfold Root of the Principle of Sufficient Reason (1813)
Originally Schopenhauer's PhD dissertation. It is a critique of the assumption that the universe is explicable or amenable to rational reflection.

The World as Will and Representation (1819)
Schopenhauer's masterpiece. He takes it that the underlying nature of the empirical world consists in blind willing. If one looks deeply enough into oneself, one discovers not only one's true inner nature, but the essence of everything.

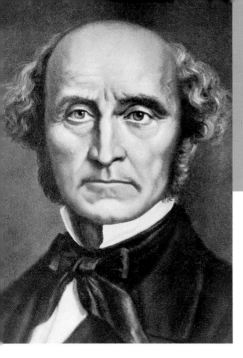

John Stuart Mill

John Stuart Mill's (1806–73) father, James Mill, was an outspoken advocate of utilitarianism and a friend of Jeremy Bentham, its founder. John Mill was born into a household steeped in utilitarian thinking, particularly Bentham's views on education.

1806–73

IT WAS THE AIM OF MILL'S FATHER TO EDUCATE THE BOY HIMSELF, in his own words, to turn him into 'a mere calculating machine'. This James Mill more or less did, with alarming consequences.

John Mill could read Greek at the age of 3 and Latin at 8. According to his autobiography, by his early teens he had read all the major Greek and Latin works, made an extensive survey of history and become well versed in jurisprudence, psychology, economics, mathematics and logic. His father lectured to him on such subjects during long walks, requiring him to write up the lectures for the father's consideration the next day. James Mill based a book, *Elements of Political Economy*, on a set of these papers. John Mill was just 14 at the time.

At 15, Mill read *Theory of Legislation*, the first published account of **Bentham**'s utilitarian views. The book changed him comprehensively: 'I felt taken up to an eminence from which I could survey a vast mental domain, and see stretching out into the distance intellectual results beyond all computation.' It gave Mill a standpoint, a philosophical position rich enough to underpin views across the philosophical spectrum, and, he hoped, the means to improve human life generally. His whole life really had prepared him for just this revelation. 'When I laid down the last volume of the [*Theory*],' he says with some reverence, 'I had become a different being.' In addition to pursuing the study of law, the new Mill spent the remainder of his teens editing many of Bentham's unpublished manuscripts, contributing to several journals with papers on current events, political debates and law, all from the utilitarian point of view.

At 20, perhaps predictably, the calculating machine suffered the worst of a series of nervous breakdowns, or at least deep bouts of depression. Already in a 'dull state of nerves', Mill reflected critically on his own happiness. He asked himself if he actually would be happy if all his aims were realized, if all his planned improvements to institutions and law were affected. On discovering that not even this could please him, he plummeted into a kind of hopeless anguish. Mill had been well-prepared for argumentation and analysis, but it seems he had no training to help him cope with the vagaries of emotion. It will send a Freudian chill down your spine to learn that he was brought out of this depression while reading about a boy who became an inspiration to his family following the death of his father. It perked Mill up, and he returned to his work, supplementing it with a new interest in poetry, culture and the arts which, it seems, formed a part of the cure too.

Utilitarianism

Mill became probably the foremost English-speaking thinker in the nineteenth century, and certainly he is among the most influential and wide-ranging. In addition to studies of jurisprudence, economics and psychology, his philosophical work spans analyses of language, logic and mathematicss, as well as scientific methodology. He has clear views on the relationship between inner mental states and the external world, formulating the first expression of phenomenalism, the view that physical objects are permanent possibilities of perception. It is, however, his writings in ethics and politics which have received the most attention, most notably *Utilitarianism* and *On Liberty*.

Mill's general aim in *Utilitarianism* is to defend and expand upon Bentham's view that good acts are those which produce the greatest happiness for the greatest number of people. Happiness is construed here, as it is in Bentham's writings, in terms of the intrinsic worth of pleasure. Although the book is a complicated one, we'll consider just one aspect of Mill's defence and one aspect of Mill's expansion on Bentham's conception of utilitarianism.

Suppose we think along the following lines, like a good utilitarian. Acts which produce the greatest happiness for the greatest number are good. It is the end, happiness, which makes actions good. Happiness itself is understood in terms of pleasure, and it is pleasure which has a special sort of value for the utilitarian. What proof have we that pleasure has this sort of value, the sort of value which carries a moral consequence, namely, that we ought to pursue it as an end? In one of the most perplexing passages in the book, Mill seems to offer the following proof:

> The sole evidence it is possible to produce that anything is desirable, is that people do actually desire it. If the end which the utilitarian doctrine proposes to itself were not, in theory and in practice, acknowledged to be an end, nothing could ever convince any person that it was so.

The claim seems to be that pleasure is actually desired by everyone, so it is, therefore, desirable, valuable in the required way for a moral demand, something we ought to pursue. Mill goes on to say that the only things visible are things seen; the only things audible are things heard. Similarly, the only things desirable are things desired, and what everyone desires is pleasure. First of all, it is not clear that the analogy works. Visible things are things which can be seen; audible things are things which can be heard. Mill needs it to be true that things desired are things which *ought* to be desired, not things which *can* be desired. As **Russell** puts it, the argument is 'so fallacious that it is hard to understand how he can have thought it valid'.

After all Mill is proposing a moral system: everyone ought to act in such a way that actions bring about a greater balance of pleasure over pain. The proof of the claim that people ought to desire pleasure cannot be just that people do desire pleasure. We cannot infer what ought to be the case from what actually is the case. Further, what becomes of the moral weight of utilitarianism if it turns out that Mill is right? What is the point of arguing that people ought to desire pleasure if they are going to desire pleasure anyway?

Second, is it true that people in fact desire pleasure? For Mill's line of argument to work, it has to be true that when I desire something, I desire that thing because of the pleasure getting it will give me. My desire, really, is for pleasure. This may sometimes be so, but when I desire a beer, for example, I really do desire the beer first and foremost – the pleasure is, for me, a secondary thing. You can complicate the question if you like by thinking about the possibility of individuals who explicitly deny that they desire pleasure. A masochist might tell you that they desire pain, maybe muddying the waters by explaining that they derive pleasure in a secondary way from their ultimate desire, pain.

Mill's expansion on Bentham's conception of utilitarianism consists in part in a consideration of not just the quantity of pleasure derived from an action, but its quality. Bentham's hedonistic calculus, complex as it was, does provide an algorithm for choosing between actions on the basis of the amount of pleasure produced, but it does not take account of distinctions between the quality of different pleasures. Mill takes it that some pleasures are of a finer quality than others, and further that such higher pleasures are more desirable than others. Why think the so-called 'higher pleasures' are more valuable than the base ones? Further, is there a clear way to tell the difference between them? Mill's answers might be gleaned from this passage:

> Few human creatures would consent to be changed into any of the lower animals, for the promise of the fullest allowance of a beast's pleasures; no intelligent human being would consent to be a fool, no instructed person would be an ignoramus, no person of feeling and conscience would be selfish and base, even though they should be persuaded that the fool, the dunce, or the rascal is better satisfied with his lot than they are with theirs.

MAJOR WORKS

System of Logic (1843)
An expression of Mill's radical empiricism. In it he argues that even the laws of logic are empirical in nature. The work also includes an important consideration of induction.

On Liberty (1859)
Deals with the conflict between minority rights and the rule of a democratic government. It contains the excellent suggestion that an individual ought not be compelled by a government to do something merely for his own good.

Utilitarianism 1861)
Mill's attempt to expand upon Bentham's conception of utilitarianism. In particular, Mill offers a treatment of the qualitative aspects of pleasure and pain.

Mill's claim here is that a person who has experienced both back rubs and poetry, both a full stomach and Mozart, will notice something having to do with the purity, sublimity, depth and refinement of higher pleasures which leaves base pleasures far behind, no matter the quantity. A person who has experienced both sorts of pleasure will be able to tell the difference between them and see that one is of a different and preferable kind to the other.

You will recall that Mill cured his depression, in part, with the finer things in life, and it might be that this clouds his judgement. He seems to be saying that the painful life of a dissatisfied intellectual is to be preferred to an idiot's life of simple pleasures. Is this compatible, at all, with the principle of utility?

Much of what Mill claims in *On Liberty* clearly follows from reflections on utilitarian principles coupled with Mill's view of what is best in us, our capacity for self-improvement and the determination of our own routes to happiness. Mill maintains that self-development, individuals pursuing their own aims, is among 'the essentials of human well-being'. Thus, individual liberty gets star billing in Mill's politics. He argues for the following curb on the powers of government: '… the only purpose for which power can rightfully be exercised over any member of a civilized community, against his will, is to prevent harm to others. His own good, either physical or moral, is not a sufficient warrant.'

It is possible to wonder just how far Mill departs from Bentham in this connection. Bentham's initial aim in working out the principle of utility was to provide lawmakers with a way of coming to reasoned conclusions about what is best for everyone. A Benthamite lawmaker ought to formulate laws for the good of the citizens, ought to curb individual activities in an effort to make the citizenry happier. Mill denies this explicitly. People should be able to do what they like, even to the extent of jeopardizing their own happiness, so long as they harm no one else.

Mill seems to be saying the life of a dissatisfied intellectual is to be preferred to an idiot's life of simple pleasures.

This is not as far from the letter of utilitarianism as one might think. Mill maintained that the state which adopts this principle has happier people in it than one which does not. Given the alarmingly comprehensive powers of modern states over their citizenry, and the regular attempt on the part of such states to justify their more dubious activities in terms of what is best for us, it is hard not to think Mill was right to want to restrict political power in this way.

Higher pleasures; to compel an individual to do something simply for their own good, says Mill in On Liberty, *is an abuse of democracy. Many would maintain that the same holds true for compelling people to refrain from – potentially – harmful actions*

Søren Kierkegaard

Soren Kierkegaard (1813–55) is generally recognized as the first existentialist philosopher. Unlike many other existentialists, there is a strong theological vein running through his philosophy.

KIERKEGAARD'S LIFE WAS IN MANY RESPECTS UNREMARKABLE – for example, he only ever left his native Denmark on three occasions, and his leisure time was spent mainly visiting the theatre and walking in Copenhagen – yet it is not possible to appreciate his work properly without knowing something about his biography. Fortunately for us, Kierkegaard kept voluminous journals from the age of twenty-one, which help with the task of understanding how his life and philosophy connect together.

He was born on 5 May 1813 in Copenhagen, and was the youngest child of Michael Kierkegaard, an affluent Danish businessman, and Ane Sørensdatter Lund, the one-time maid of his father's first wife. His father, the most significant figure of his youth, was a deeply religious man who was committed to a particularly pietistic form of Lutheranism, and was racked with chronic feelings of anxiety and guilt. Some commentators locate the source of these feelings in an incident from his childhood where he had cursed God from the top of a hill after he had become exhausted and cold whilst tending sheep, while others point to the possibility that he impregnated his second wife before he married her. Whatever the truth of the matter, he passed on his pessimistic and gloomy religious outlook to his son, who later described his upbringing as 'insane' and wrote in a journal entry that he had come into the world as the result of a 'crime'.

The sense of foreboding which permeated Kierkegaard's early years was compounded by the premature deaths of his mother and five of his brothers and sisters. It was his father's belief that this was a sign of divine retribution; indeed, he did not expect any of his children to survive beyond the age of 34, and with the exceptions of Søren and Peter, his eldest son, he was proved right.

Given this background, Kierkegaard's education was surprisingly normal; he attended a celebrated private school – Borgedydskolen – where he was lonely, aloof and intellectually the superior of his classmates; and then, at the age of 17, he went to the University of Copenhagen with the aim of studying theology. This didn't quite go to plan. There followed a brief period of what passed for teenage rebellion in nineteenth-century Denmark. At university, Kierkegaard became more interested in philosophy and literature than theology; and he adopted the lifestyle of a party animal, drinking, smoking and running up debts which his father then had to settle.

Ethics and Aesthetics

However, in 1838 his father died, and this seems to have brought an end to Kierkegaard's career as a bon vivant. He turned his attention back to his theological studies, and two years later gained his master's degree. It was also at this time that he became involved with Regine Olsen in the only real love affair of his life. As is well documented in his journals, he proposed to her, immediately regretted it, spent a year equivocating, and eventually broke off the engagement in 1841. The reasons for his behaviour are not entirely clear; however, it seems that he came to the view that his melancholic temperament was unsuited to marriage; that he was intellectually incompatible with her; and that his vocation as a writer meant that he could not commit himself to marriage.

It is clear that the affair profoundly affected him. It crops up time and again in his journals, and also appears, thinly disguised, in his philosophical works. For example, he uses parts of *Either/Or*, one of his first major publications, to work through the various issues which motivated his decision to break with Regine. Similarly, another early work, *Repetition*, tells the story of a young man unable to marry the woman he loves because he fears the ethical commitment which marriage requires. Of course, there is more to these works than merely the effort to exorcize a few psychological demons; they also have serious philosophical points to make.

In *Either/Or*, he sets out two modes of existence by which people might live their lives. The first, the aesthetic mode, which is articulated in the papers and letters of a person called 'A', is hedonistic in character, emphasizing the importance of immediate gratification and living in the moment. The ethical mode, in contrast, is built on duty and obligation. It is conveyed in two letters to 'A' that analyse and criticize his motives and prospects, and suggest that in order to achieve fulfilment he should commit himself to the kinds of continuous projects which would constitute an ethical life. Kierkegaard's own view about the right choice here was

MAJOR WORKS

Either/Or (1843)

Sets out a view of two modes of life, the 'aesthetic' and the 'ethical'. The aesthetic is hedonistic in character, emphasising the importance of immediate gratification and living in the moment. The ethical mode, in contrast, is built on duty and obligation. Kierkegaard came to the view that neither mode of life was satisfactory.

Repetition (1843)

This work tells the story of a young man unable to marry the woman he loves, since he fears the ethical commitment which marriage requires. Clearly, influenced by Kierkegaard's doomed affair with Regine Olson.

Fear and Trembling (1843)

An analysis of the conflict between the demands of ethics and religion, strikingly illustrated by the story of Abraham, required by God to kill his son. Kierkegaard argues that to obey this instruction requires behaviour which is completely outside the domain of normal morals; it necessitates a suspension of the ethical in the service of a higher telos (goal).

The Concept of Anxiety (1844)

This work focuses on the pervasiveness of anxiety in the stage of life which precedes religious faith. It makes the claim that anxiety is linked to an awareness of human freedom, the inevitability of sin and the requirement of radical choice.

disguised by his use of unusual narrative techniques and multiple pseudonyms. However, he quickly came to the view that neither the aesthetic, nor the ethical mode, were adequate; rather there existed a third mode of existence, the religious sphere, where humans might find true freedom and fulfilment.

The Leap of Faith

The religious sphere is constituted by a 'leap of faith', made in 'fear and trembling', which takes it outside the domain of rationality. The Christian's worship of the God-man Jesus, who is both temporal and eternal, is necessarily paradoxical. It is simply not possible to appeal to rational argument or empirical evidence to justify such a belief; all that is available is passionate commitment. In his book *Fear and Trembling*, Kierkegaard spells out what this might mean for ethics by looking at the biblical story of Abraham and Isaac.

In Genesis, the first book of the Bible, God commands Abraham to kill his son Isaac. According to Kierkegaard, obeying this instruction requires behaviour which is completely outside the domain of normal morals; it necessitates a suspension of the ethical in the service of a higher *telos* (goal). He illustrates this by comparing the situation of Abraham to that of a 'tragic hero'. To take a modern example, consider the following scenario: A military commander knows that if she wants to prevent the destruction of a city, then she must send a battalion of her soldiers to their certain deaths; the battalion includes amongst its number her son. This constitutes a very difficult moral dilemma, but it lends itself to rational discussion; whatever course of action the commander chooses, she will be able to offer a justification for it which other people will understand. This is not the case with Abraham. He must simply follow a command, which comes to him from above, that will have a consequence that is absolutely unthinkable in terms of normal moral discourse. Not only can he not justify his actions to other people, he cannot even tell himself a story to explain why it is required of him. All that counts is his passionate commitment to a subjective, felt relationship with God.

Religious faith then is not an easy option, and indeed, according to Kierkegaard, proper religious faith can only be achieved with great difficulty. So why choose it? Why not remain wedded to the aesthetic and ethical modes of existence? The answer is that it is only by religious faith that individuals can avoid despair and find their true selves in the freedom which, paradoxically, dependence upon a transcendent being brings.

In emphasizing the irrational and subjective dimensions of the religious mode of existence, Kierkegaard is also making a wider point about the futility of attempts to achieve objective knowledge of the totality of human thought and experience by the means of a rational, logical, systematic, metaphysical framework. His particular target here is Hegelianism, which, in the middle part of the nineteenth century, was the dominant philosophical approach in Denmark. In its totalizing imperative, Hegelianism is necessarily flawed; for example, with respect to religion, it aims to make God and the Christian faith transparent to reason, whereas in fact they remain necessarily outside the domain of rational understanding.

This also ties in with the unusual way in which Kierkegaard presents his arguments. Nearly all of his important philosophical works were published pseudonymously; they also make heavy use of irony, satire and humour to make

Abraham prepares willingly to sacrifice his son Isaac, in obedience to God's command. According to Kierkegaard, religious observance such as this lies outside the realm of everyday morals, necessitating a suspension of ethical judgement.

their points. This was in the service of a method Kierkegaard called 'indirect communication'. The idea was to deprive his readers of the comforts of authorial authority, thereby compelling them to make their own judgements about where they stood on particular issues and arguments. Kierkegaard drew a link here with the way that **Socrates** encouraged his interlocutors to think for themselves by undermining their standard responses to the questions he asked. This method is driven by his on-going commitment to the importance of individual choice and responsibility.

Kierkegaard always recognized that his work would not find favour whilst he was alive; indeed, he predicted that it would only be in the twentieth century that the significance of his writings would be appreciated. He was largely right. The first book written about him was not published until 1877, 22 years after his death at the age of 42; and although he became well known in Germany in the early part of the twentieth century, it wasn't really until the period between the two world wars that he became considered to be a major intellectual figure. Obviously, the emergence of existentialism had a lot to do with this, because the themes which Kierkegaard examined in his work are similar to those which were explored by philosophers like **Heidegger** and **Sartre**. Particularly, his emphasis on the importance of individual freedom and the responsibilities and burdens which it brings, is a thread which runs through nearly all existentialist thought.

Of course, not everybody has good things to say about Kierkegaard. There is, for example, the suspicion that the core of irrationality which lies at the heart of his philosophy is all too easily transfigured into a kind of nihilism, or even fascism. After all, as **Voltaire** made only too clear, many terrible things have been justified on the basis of appeals to faith (and, indeed, Kierkegaard himself had some pretty reactionary social views). Nevertheless, his importance as a philosopher is without question; by insisting that individuals and subjectivity, freedom and passion, are important, he helped to bring philosophy down from the clouds, where it had been in danger of floating off on a Hegelian wind.

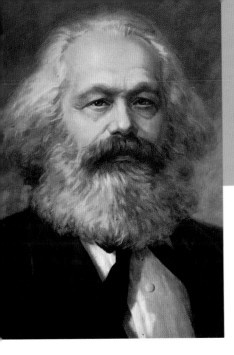

Karl Marx

By some measures, Karl Marx (1818–1883) is the most important of the modern philosophers, in the sense that is impossible to understand the history of the twentieth century without reference to his ideas.

THE REVOLUTIONS IN RUSSIA AND CHINA WERE BOTH, AT LEAST OSTENSIBLY, Marxist in character. The Second World War turned out in favour of the Allies partly because Hitler, blinded by his hatred of communism, ordered an invasion of the Soviet Union. And the Cold War pitched Western-style capitalism against societies which identified themselves as socialist or communist.

Marx's influence, of course, is not a matter of pure happenstance. He wrote with the intention of changing the world. Thus, his *Communist Manifesto*, written with his friend Friedrich Engels, ends with a call to arms:

> The Communists disdain to conceal their views and aims. They openly declare that their ends can be attained only by the forcible overthrow of all existing social conditions. Let the ruling classes tremble at a communist revolution. The proletarians have nothing to lose but their chains. They have a world to win. Workers of all countries, unite!

There was little in Marx's early life to suggest that he would become modernity's exemplary political radical. He was born on 5 May 1818 in the city of Trier on the banks of the Mosel. His father, Heinrich Marx, was an interesting fellow. A successful lawyer, he converted from Judaism to Christianity shortly before Karl was born, largely to protect his business from Prussian anti-Semitism. Heinrich was a disciple of the Enlightenment, and he introduced Karl to the writings of great Enlightenment thinkers, such as **Leibniz**, **Voltaire** and **Kant**, and also to liberal political ideas.

The young Marx was a forceful personality. His sisters later recounted how he bullied them relentlessly, but made up for it by reading them stories. He shone at school in literary subjects – though he wasn't so good at mathematics and history – and it was the intention that he should follow in his father's footsteps and become a lawyer, and so, in 1835, he went off to the University of Bonn to study law. But a year later, he moved to the University of Berlin, switched from law to philosophy and hooked up with a group of radical thinkers, members of the Young Hegelian *Doktorklub*. It was at this point that Marx's radicalism came to the fore. He identified himself as left-wing; committed himself to democratic politics and espoused atheism.

Unfortunately for Marx, his newly found radicalism put paid to any hopes of finding an academic job. In 1842, having successfully completed his doctorate, he began the first of a number of jobs editing radical journals. The next few years were probably the most important in the development of his thought. Crucially, in 1844 he began a lifelong friendship with Friedrich Engels (1820–95), the son of a textile manufacturer. It was Engels who introduced Marx to the emergent working-class movement, and also to the study of political economy. This point marks the emergence of a recognizably Marxist social and political philosophy.

It is sensible to strike a cautionary note here. Marx was not straightforwardly a philosopher. It would perhaps be more accurate to describe him as a social or political theorist. His inclusion in a book of this sort is warranted, first, because his work is steeped in philosophy; and second, because he has influenced many philosophers, particularly those working in continental Europe. However, the fact that his work covers a broad range of subject areas – philosophy, economics, political theory and history, amongst others – makes it hard to summarize. Or rather, it means that any summary will be necessarily selective. But having said that, it is certainly possible to identify some of the key themes in Marx's thought.

Marx and Human Nature

Perhaps the best jumping off point if we want to understand Marxist theory is to consider how Marx viewed human beings. In other words, did he have a theory of human nature? The answer to this question is an equivocal yes. Marx did not think of human nature in the same terms as, say, a contemporary sociobiologist; he was not, for example, interested in the specification of particular human instincts. But he did think that it was in the nature of human beings to cooperate in a process of collective, freely chosen labour. His idea was that humans come to full self-realization in the process of transforming the world in their own image through their labour. This is quite a complicated notion – which is not surprising, given that it has an antecedent in the philosophy of Georg **Hegel** – but perhaps a sense of it can be attained by imagining a team of engineers who put body and soul into producing a fantastic building; when they subsequently gaze at the building, it isn't too fanciful to think that they see something of their own humanity, of their productive sociality, in their creation.

Marx did think that it was in the nature of humans to cooperate in a process of collective, freely-chosen labour.

The importance of this idea that human beings come to full self-realization through freely chosen labour is that it underpins the concept of alienation, which in turn is the lynchpin of Marx's criticism of societies that are characterized by class conflict. Put simply, people are alienated when they are separated from the products of their labour and from the labour process itself. This occurs when they lose control over the circumstances in which they engage in productive activity and over the products of their labour. The key point about alienation is that it is always self-alienation. For Marx, to be alienated is to be separated from one's essential humanity; it is to be unable to live a fully human life.

Self and Alienation

Alienation, in varying degrees, is a facet of all class societies; that is, all societies where there is a division between those people who own and control the means of production and those who do not. However, it is in capitalist societies that alienation reaches its zenith. Capitalism is characterized by a fundamental conflict between two great, antagonistic classes, the bourgeoisie, the owners of the means of production (i.e. factories, machinery, etc.), and the proletariat, who own only their own labour power. The proletariat are alienated because they are forced to sell their labour under circumstances not of their own choosing. They have little or no control over the labour process, and their productive energies are expended for the benefit of the class which exploits them. Marx describes the proletarian's experience of alienation thus:

> ...he does not fulfil himself in his work but denies himself, has a feeling of misery rather than well-being, does not develop freely his mental and physical energies but is physically exhausted and mentally debased. The worker, therefore, feels himself at home only during his leisure time, whereas at work he feels homeless. His work is not voluntary but imposed, forced labour. It is not the satisfaction of a need, but only a means for satisfying other needs.

The House of Trade Unions in Moscow, with multilingual proclamations and banners of 'fathers' of the Marxist state, Marx, Engels, Lenin and Stalin during the Stalin era.

However, all is not lost for the proletariat, for it was Marx's view that they are the bearers of the emancipatory potential of humankind. Capitalism is not indestructible; indeed, according to Marx, it is riddled with contradictions, which in the end will result in its downfall; and it is the proletariat who will bring this about. Specifically, as a *class-for-itself*, a class aware of its own reality and situation, it is the destiny of the proletariat to abolish all class distinctions, instituting a new form of society – communism – based on collective ownership; in doing so, they will end the alienation of people from the products of their labour, from the labour process itself, and from their essential humanity.

At this point, the Marxist account runs into difficulties; capitalism is still going strong, and the proletariat, if they exist, do not seem to be aware that they are supposed to be a revolutionary force. So what's gone wrong? Was Marx just incorrect about all this?

It is possible to be charitable here. Marx was aware that capitalism had resources at its disposal to allow it to counter the effects of its internal contradictions. For example, you'll find that Marxists make a big play about something they call 'false class consciousness'. The idea here is that the working class are not aware of their historic destiny as a revolutionary force because they have been exposed to capitalist ideology. The bourgeoisie, as a result of their domination of the economic sphere, also control things like the educational system and the mass media. Therefore, they are able to get their ideas out into society at large, with the result that the proletariat remain blind to their true situation. In Marxist parlance, the proletariat never make the transition from a *class-in-itself* to a *class-for-itself*.

It is, of course, also possible to argue that capitalism has not crumbled yet, but that it will; that Marx might have been wrong about timescales, but that he got the fundamentals right. This kind of argument is often coupled with an analysis of the way in which capitalist economies have managed to exploit new markets, for example, in the developing world. However, there is something philosophically suspect about this move; the claim that something has not happened yet, but that it is sure to happen at some point in the future is unfalsifiable and there is more than a whiff of blind faith about it.

Moreover, it isn't clear that Marxism is rescued even if one grants that capitalism might one day come to an end. The problem is that the Marxist idea that capitalism will be replaced by a society free of systematic inequality and conflict just isn't very plausible. Perhaps wisely, Marx didn't have a lot to say about the precise form that communism would take. He suggested that people in communist society – rational, self-aware and other-directed – would no longer be estranged from each other or themselves. His friend Engels envisaged a day when state power and the government of people would not be necessary.

The question is whether, from the perspective of the twenty-first century, this is a plausible vision of the future. Probably it isn't. But having said that, it is perhaps slightly unfair to hold Marx up to the standards of twenty-first century knowledge when accusing him of flawed understanding. Not least, he had not experienced the horrors of the twentieth century when putting his theories together. It is not implausible to think that with the kind of hindsight that the last century leaves us with, Marx might have been less optimistic about human potential and the possibilities for a world without fundamental conflict.

MAJOR WORKS

Paris Manuscripts (1844)
A series of extracts on philosophy and economics, primarily notable for the first proper expression of Marx's ideas on alienation.

German Ideology (1846)
Co-written with Friedrich Engels, and published only posthumously, the doctrine of historical materialism was first expounded in this work.

The Communist Manifesto (1848)
Classic and polemical statement of Marx's revolutionary philosophy of history, it became the manifesto of many a communist party. It pursues the political implications of the fact that 'the history of all hitherto existing societies is the history of class struggle'.

A Contribution to the Critique of Political Economy (1859)
Noted for its Preface, which is a succinct expression of the materialist philosophy of history.

Capital (3 Volumes: 1867, 1884, 1893)
Marx's definitive and most famous work, still uncompleted at his death. Primarily a work of political economy, it constitutes an exhaustive account of the workings, and failings, of capitalist society. The second and third volumes were edited and published by Friedrich Engels.

Charles Sanders Peirce

Charles Sanders Peirce (1839–1914) was unusual for a philosopher in that he published no major work outlining his thought. Nevertheless, his contributions to the subject are immense, if not yet fully realized.

PEIRCE IS BEST KNOWN AS THE FOUNDER OF PRAGMATISM, or, as he later came to call it, in order to distinguish it properly, 'pragmaticism'. However, it would be a mistake to suppose that this was the extent of his intellectual interests, since he also wrote prolifically on subjects as diverse as mathematics, economics, anthropology, the history of science, language, psychology, and more. Indeed, his published output runs to some twelve thousand pages, and there are at least a further eighty thousand extant pages which have yet to be published.

Peirce, the son of Harvard mathematician Benjamin Peirce, was born in Cambridge, Massachusetts, in September 1839. He was brought up in an atmosphere of intellectual excellence which befitted his father's status as one of the country's most esteemed mathematicians. Some of the top scientific and philosophical thinkers of the time were regular visitors to the Peirce household, and Charles was encouraged to be intellectually curious and independent from a very early age. Benjamin Peirce took responsibility for his son's education, and many commentators attribute Peirce's originality to the didactic techniques his father employed. His normal method was to set Charles some problem to solve, to leave him to it, and then simply to check his solution.

As with many of the great philosophers, Peirce showed his abilities very early in life; by the age of eight, for example, he was studying chemistry, and at 13 he started to read **Kant**'s *Critique of Pure Reason*. However, he didn't do particularly well as an undergraduate at Harvard, reportedly because he found things too easy to be interesting, coming only seventy-ninth out of a class of ninety. He was soon to show his abilities, though, when he was the first student to graduate *summa cum laude* from Harvard's Lawrence Scientific School.

His next move turned out to be very important in shaping the tenor of his philosophy; he went to work for the United States Coast and Geodetic Survey, with which he was to be associated for 30 years. The significance of this is that Peirce saw himself as, and indeed for much of the time was, a practising scientist, which is reflected in the concerns which drive his work. Thus, for example, he called his pragmatism the philosophy of the laboratory scientist.

Peirce saw himself very much as a scientist, naming his pragmatism the 'philosophy of the laboratory scientist'.

The Essence of Pragmatism

The central contention of pragmatism is summed up in a statement from his article 'How to Make Our Ideas Clear', which was published in *Popular Science Monthly* in 1878: 'Consider what effects, that might conceivably have practical bearings, we conceive the object of our conception to have. Then, our conception of these effects is the whole of our conception of the object.'

In essence, what is being claimed here is that we get clarity about the content of a thought or concept by discerning, under a multitude of different conditions, its various real-world instantiations. Or, to put this another way, clarity comes by working through the experimental consequences of the content of a thought or concept.

Peirce illustrates this idea with reference to the concepts 'hard' and 'heavy':

> [L]et us ask what we mean by calling a thing *hard*. Evidently that it will not be scratched by many other substances. The whole conception of this quality, as of every other, lies in its conceived effects. There is absolutely no difference between a hard thing and a soft thing so long as they are not brought to the test. ('How to Make Our Ideas Clear')
>
> To say that a body is heavy means simply that, in the absence of opposing force, it will fall. This (neglecting certain specifications of how it will fall, etc., which exist in the mind of the physicist who uses the word) is evidently the whole conception of weight. ('How to Make Our Ideas Clear')

Thus, the concept 'hard' gets its meaning from the things which happen when we put hard objects to the test; for example, they don't scratch, they don't crumble when touched, they will dent soft objects, and so on. And similarly with heavy things; they fall when not supported.

A Definition of Truth

For Peirce this idea has some radical consequences; most particularly it led him to define truth as that about which there is a long-term consensus of opinion amongst a community of responsible inquirers. The idea here is that on any given issue all investigators will eventually come to the same conclusion. This happens because real things have the effect of causing beliefs; therefore, given that there is only one reality, the beliefs of a community of responsible inquirers will eventually accord both with it and with each other:

> Different minds may set out with the most antagonistic views, but the progress of investigation carries them by a force outside of themselves to one and the same conclusion. This activity of thought by which we are carried, not where we wish, but to a fore-ordained goal, is like the operation of destiny. No modification of the point of view taken, no selection of other facts for study, no natural bent of mind even, can enable a man to escape the predestinate opinion ... The opinion which is *fated* to be ultimately agreed to by all who investigate, is what we mean by the truth, and the object represented in this opinion is the real. That is the way I would explain reality. ('How to Make Our Ideas Clear')

This idea is not without its problems. For example, it has been pointed out that there appears to be a strange contradiction in the argument. Reality is said to control and drive people's beliefs; yet reality itself is constituted by a long-term consensus of agreement. Therefore, it seems that consensual opinion is driving people towards consensual opinion!

Though there may be logical problems with Peirce's conception of truth, these do not significantly impact on the way in which he saw science in practice as proceeding. He was committed to a thoroughly fallibilistic conception of scientific methodology, that is, he saw science as progressing by means of the testing of propositions derived from hypotheses about the nature of the world.

In fact, in a fashion which anticipated more modern notions of scientific method, he saw scientific enquiry as proceeding according to three principles of inference: first, abduction, which refers to the generation of hypotheses for the purposes of explaining particular phenomena; second, deduction, which is the mechanism by which testable propositions are derived from hypotheses; and third, inference, which is the whole process of experimentation which takes place in order to test hypotheses.

Peirce was aware that in proposing a fallibilistic account of scientific progress, he was committed to the view that scientific truths are necessarily provisional. Indeed, he came to argue that one should never be committed to the truth of current scientific opinion, but rather merely accept it as a stage on the way towards truth. However, somewhat paradoxically, in line with his idea that reality is constituted by the long-term consensus of a community of inquirers, he was optimistic about the possibility of attaining final answers to particular questions. Indeed, so long as questions had genuinely testable consequences, then the truth about them would eventually be known.

A Logical Turn

Peirce's ideas about pragmatism and scientific knowledge were outlined in articles written in the late 1870s. After this time, he turned his attention to logic, and with his students in 1883, he published *Studies in Logic*, which contained his version of the logic of what is called quantification. However, its publication coincided with a downturn in his fortunes. In 1884, he was effectively sacked from his university position, apparently after information about his errant behaviour – he was widely perceived to be a libertine of dubious morality and unorthodox religious beliefs – came to the notice of the university authorities; and in 1891 his job at the United States Costal Survey also disappeared. This plunged him into poverty. Indeed, now living with his second wife in near-seclusion in Pennsylvania, and considered unemployable inside academia, he was dependent on occasional consulting work and the goodwill of friends like William **James** for his survival.

When Peirce died in 1914, his death went largely unnoticed in the philosophical community. However, since then, and particularly with the publication of the

MAJOR WORKS

Peirce did not publish any single philosophical work summarising or explicating his philosophical position, preferring instead to write technical articles for academic journals. Interested readers, therefore, would be best advised to consult a volume of his collected works, perhaps Houser and Kloesel's two volume, *The Essential Peirce* (Indiana University Press). Of the many secondary sources available, *The Cambridge Companion to Peirce* (Cambrige University Press) is perhaps the best starting point.

Philosophy of the laboratory scientist; Peirce believed that truth was provisional, and had to be constantly reassessed in the light of the results of new experimentation.

first volume of his collected papers in the 1930s, his reputation has undergone a renaissance. In this outline of his life and work, we have concentrated on his pragmatim and his ideas about science. However, for the professional philosopher, other areas of his work are of equal importance. In particular, he did interesting and original work on logic, semiotics and metaphysics. His significance as an intellectual figure is now coming to be fully appreciated. Max H. Fisch puts it like this:

> Who is the most original and the most versatile intellect that the Americas have so far produced? The answer 'Charles S. Peirce' is uncontested … [He was] mathematician, astronomer, chemist, geodesist, surveyor, cartographer, metrologist, spectroscopist, engineer, inventor; psychologist, philologist, lexicographer, historian of science, mathematical economist, lifelong student of medicine; book reviewer, dramatist, actor, short story writer; phenomenologist, semiotician, logician, rhetorician and metaphysician.

All this, and yet with some eighty thousand pages of his work still to be published, there is presumably more to come. It is fair to say then that Peirce lived up to his early promise.

William James

William James (1842–1910) was the brother of the novelist Henry James. Along with C.S Peirce, James would achieve his own recognition with the founding of the first home-grown American school of philosophy, pragmatism.

IN 1905, WILLIAM JAMES (1842–1910) RECORDED THE FOLLOWING ENTRIES in his diary, as he considered the possibility of retiring from professional teaching: October 26th, 'Resign!'; 28th, 'Resign!!!'; November 4th, 'Resign?'; 7th, 'Resign!'; 8th, 'Don't resign'; 9th, 'Resign!'; 16th, 'Don't resign!'; 23rd, 'Resign'; December 7th, 'Don't resign'; 9th, 'Teach here next year.' He continued at Harvard until somehow managing to resign in 1907. You can form the impression from this, probably rightly, that James's mind moved in several directions at once. Possibly this trait nearly killed him, but the resolution he came to became pragmatism, the first home-grown American philosophical movement.

Many commentators trace James's breath-taking indecisiveness to the fact that he spent his childhood in a kind of benevolent upheaval. James's grandfather, an Irish immigrant, was a multi-millionaire, and, following his death, James's father Henry enjoyed financial independence. This was probably just as well, as Henry James was something of a restless intellectual, with religious aspirations but no head for business, and the income enabled him to pursue his interests and devote himself to his children's education. The five children – James's brother Henry was the well-known novelist – were taught to think freely and fiercely, with breakfast table discussion ranging as widely as their interests carried them. The family moved regularly back and forth between the United States and Europe, largely with the aim of gaining the best possible education for the children. They spoke many languages between them and had a decidedly cosmopolitan tolerance for the beliefs of others. James was able to see virtually every side of every argument or possible choice, the merits and disadvantages of all.

While this is usually an attractive character trait, it led to James's near-paralysis with respect to life choices. James suffered from insomnia, bad eyesight and back problems all his life, but there was also always an undercurrent of depression compounding the physical misery. Some argue that his depression grew from his inability to come to the conclusion that what he was doing with his life was right in the face of the many alternatives his disposition easily brought into view. His family moved to Rhode Island so that James could study art – some of his excellent portraits survive and are worth a look – but he dropped it within a year and enrolled in the Lawrence Scientific School at Harvard. Still unsure that the laboratory bench was the right place for him, he took a place at the Harvard Medical School. He interrupted this with a year-long expedition to the Amazon with the bizarre anthropologist Louis Agassiz. He found himself nearly middle-aged and with no clear idea of what to do with his life.

On Determinism

This uncomfortable feeling was made worse by philosophical worries about the possible truth of determinism. What difference could a life make if every action, thought and hope were caused by prior events? What meaning could a life have at all? At the heart of his crisis, too, was a conflict between religion and science. James's father came under the influence of the dubious Emanuel Swedenborg, and spent a life working through his own conception of religious belief. No doubt James felt some pressure to adopt his father's religiosity. However, James himself, though possessed of no small artistic and literary talent, felt drawn to the hard facts of scientific enquiry. The pain of this conflict, as well as his directionless life, combined with the possibility that there was no free choice available that might lead to a resolution, was nearly too much for him. Suicide became a serious consideration.

A philosophical conversion seemed to save him. James read the work of the French philosopher Charles-Bernard Renouvier and found in it an unusual solution to the problems posed by determinism. Renouvier argues that free will consists in 'the sustaining of a thought because I choose to when I might have other thoughts'. One might not be able to choose which thoughts come into the mind, but an act of will can focus the mind on some thoughts at the expense of others, thoughts which then determine action. It led James to the view that neither the thesis of determinism nor free will is provable, leaving room for a kind of choice based on the practical consequences of adopting one or the other position. James opted for free will and, in so doing, seemed to get it. Here is a kind of kernel of pragmatism, as we shall see.

James got himself under way. He was commissioned to write a textbook on the new science of psychology. Predictably, it was published 10 years behind schedule and did not resemble a textbook in the slightest. It was *The Principles of Psychology*, and its influence was immediate, lasting and large.

Empathy on the battlefield. James argued that no matter how hard one tries, it is impossible to fully empathize with another's pain.

The book is positivist in flavour, and attempts to make the psychological study of mind a part of natural science, showing how mental life and visible bodily life are connected. The mark of the mental, for example, becomes a question of identifying the characteristic behaviour of things with minds. According to James, such things exhibit plastic or flexible goal-directed behaviour – they make choices which enable them to get what they want despite obstacles. James, under the sober influence of Darwin, is then led to reasonable reflection on the point and purpose of mind from an evolutionary point of view. Put a minded thing up against a mere automaton, and the minded thing will outperform the mechanism every time.

Perhaps the most interesting part of the book is the chapter on consciousness, which James famously characterizes as 'the stream of thought'. Breaking with the traditional view of, say, sense perception as repeatable inner images – seeing the same dead ant on your nightstand today as yesterday involves the same thing happening in conscious experience – James argues that consciousness is in a constant state of flux. Consciousness, for James, is also personal: it is owned or belongs to someone, with all the mental baggage this entails. As such, the vagaries of personal circumstance do more than just flavour experience, ensuring that the stream is always changing; circumstances make the various streams distinct. No matter what your powers of empathy are, you will never feel my pain.

James's consideration of the self broke with tradition too. Instead of talk of ghostly souls or some other substance on which to hang the draperies of personal identity – what it is which makes you you over time – he distinguishes between the 'I' and the 'me'. The material me is made up of objects to which I have a kind of emotional attachment or personal interest: family, friends and valued possessions. The social part of me consists in the roles I play in different social circumstances. Cherished values make up the spiritual me. My best hopes for me are the ideal me. The 'I' for James is closer to the usual notion of ego or self, but he identifies it with something nearly Aristotelian: a kind of activity which consists in one's present thinking.

Pragmatism

Following the publication of *The Principles of Psychology*, James seems to have all but dropped his interest in psychology for philosophy, attempting in particular to reconcile the tension he felt between the religious impulse and the hard-headed demands of scientific enquiry. The result is an articulation of pragmatism, a term borrowed from his friend **Peirce**, who argued that pragmatic concerns should guide our understanding of truth and meaning. James fleshed out the view in accord with his own concerns. His expressed contention that philosophy ought to be concerned with the lives of everyday people is responsible for another large difference between James and Peirce. James's writing is much less technical than Peirce's. With James we get a little less clarity in exchange for a lot more readability.

James's opinion of pragmatism certainly had something to do with his escape from suicide. Truth, for James, consists partly in the usefulness of an idea, and usefulness is a complex matter. The simple-minded objection to pragmatism, that it is nothing other than a free licence to believe whatever makes a person feel a little better, misses at least a part of the point. Usefulness for James depends not just on the extent to which an idea pushes one towards a better life, but also on the predictive power an idea might confer – the view is in line with James's radical empiricism. James also argues that an idea of x is only a useful idea if it helps one deal with x should x exist. Truth really does correspond to reality for the pragmatist. Further, ideas must be consistent with other ideas to stand a chance of being true. There are elements of coherentism here too.

The emphasis, though, is clearly on what difference the idea makes for practical affairs. As James puts it:

> Pragmatism asks its usual question. 'Grant an idea or belief to be true,' it says, 'what concrete difference will its being true make in anyone's actual life? How will the truth be realized? What experiences will be different from those which would obtain if the belief were false? What, in short, is the truth's cash value in experiential terms?'

The view provides a decision procedure for dealing with metaphysical disputes. To use James's example, suppose you were circling a tree, trying to have a glimpse of a squirrel who is matching your movements around the tree too. If someone asks, 'Are you going around the squirrel?' you can interpret the question in at least two ways, but what possible difference to human conduct could your answer make? Philosophical disputes are often merely linguistic in just this way. Where there's no difference for practice – no cash value – there's no difference at all.

James is subject to considerable criticism concerning his religious views. He argues that empirical evidence cannot decide the matter of God's existence, and so a part of the decision consists in plumping for the belief which most improves life. Belief in God wins, just, because it leads one to a better attitude towards the future and puts some much-needed meaning into a life.

Can one really just will to believe something like this? Apparently, James both thought so and did so. You can hear something of the escape from suicide in all of this. It certainly was James's view that philosophy should take some of the sting out of existence, as it clearly did for him. He urges us to '[b]elieve that life is worth living and your belief will help create the fact'. One can quibble with James's arguments, but it is hard to find a reason to object to his motivations.

MAJOR WORKS

The Principles of Psychology (1890)
James' long and bold treatment of mind. It includes his famous account of the stream of consciousness, the 'I' as opposed to the 'me', and free will.

The Will to Believe and Other Essays in Popular Philosophy (1897)
A collection of papers on such topics as rationality, determinism, morality and the meaning of life. It expounds James' view that some questions force a choice even when the evidence is inconclusive. On such occasions, some answers contribute to a better life than others, and this gives us a right to believe them.

The Varieties of Religious Experience (1902)
James' study of human nature, in particular, that aspect of human nature which is concerned with religious experience.

Pragmatism (1907)
A collection of lectures on the pragmatic theory of truth, meaning, knowledge and the pragmatic method of resolving philosophical questions.

Friedrich Nietzsche

Friedrich Nietzsche (1844–1900) remains one of the nineteenth century's most misunderstood and misquoted philosophers. His most notorious concept, however, that of the Superman, is in fact closer to Aristotle's man of virtue than it is to some glorified Aryan hero.

FRIEDRICH NIETZSCHE WAS INFLUENTIAL, CONTROVERSIAL, DISTURBING, systematically misunderstood and very good fun to read. It is his excellent prose that initially attracts many of us. You can easily spend an afternoon gorging on his words, by turns smiling at his wit and gasping at his dark pronouncements. You can then spend a lifetime working out his meaning.

Nietzsche's short life began on 15 October – the birthday, too, of his namesake Friedrich Wilhelm IV, the King of Prussia – in Röcken, Prussia. His father, Ludwig, was a Lutheran minister and his mother, Franziska, was the daughter of a Lutheran minister. What bearing this surfeit of Lutheranism had on his scathing treatment of religion is worth thinking about. So too is the fact that Nietzsche's father lost his mind when Nietzsche was only five – there is some speculation about the unlikely possibility that Nietzsche's insanity was inherited. Following his father's collapse, he, his sister and mother lived with the maternal side of the family: two aunts and a grandmother. Nietzsche obtained an excellent classical education in a famous boarding school and eventually took a place at the University of Bonn to study theology. He quickly abandoned theology for philology at the University of Leipzig, toying momentarily with the possibility of studying chemistry. It was at Leipzig that Nietzsche discovered his three great early influences: **Schopenhauer**, the materialist F.A. Lange and Wagner. It was also at Leipzig that Nietzsche, who seems to have otherwise abstained from sex throughout his life, probably contracted syphilis in a brothel.

Following a brief stint in the military, which was cut short due to a chest injury caused by the pommel of his saddle while he was mounting his horse with excessive exuberance, Nietzsche rather astonishingly was offered the Chair in Philology at the University of Basel. He had not completed a doctoral thesis, but the enthusiasm of his tutors and Nietzsche's great gifts carried him through to the post. He was just 24.

He soon took leave to serve as a medic in the Franco-Prussian war, and on his return to the university was plagued by dysentery and diphtheria. Although he got to work on his first book and undertook the usual teaching duties, Nietzsche was never well. He had suffered from a number of health problems since early childhood – migraines, insomnia, poor eyesight and stomach upsets, which were probably the result of ulcers. His old illnesses coupled with his new ones finally forced him to retire from the post. He spent the remainder of his sane life shambling between boarding houses in constant ill-health – with the possibility of suicide his only comfort, he once confided – writing and publishing a remarkable number of books and essays, filling countless notebooks in the process.

In January 1889 in the Piazzo Carlo Alberto in Turin, he watched as a cab driver beat his horse. Something snapped. Nietzsche flung himself around the horse's neck and eventually collapsed, utterly insane. He spent the following 11 years in a Basel asylum or in the care of his mother, until her death, and finally his sister. He never recovered. It is suspected that Nietzsche suffered from syphilitic lunacy. If this were not degradation enough, Nietzsche's unspeakable sister did much to squander her brother's legacy, and it is possible that her efforts had something to do with the disastrous appropriation of his philosophy by the Nazis. It is clear, though, that Nietzsche would have despised all of this. He certainly thought little of German nationalism in particular and party politics in general.

Truth and Values

It is not possible to work through Nietzsche's many volumes in any detail here, but we can consider some of the themes which recur in several of them. Nietzsche's writings are sometimes mistakenly regarded as lessons in nihilism, the view that values have no justification or meaning. Some take it that Nietzsche argues for the claim that there are no moral standards, that truth has no value, and that religion is decadent or dying, and certainly Nietzsche says all of this or nearly says it. Nihilism, though, is not his conclusion; it's his starting point. He argues that the West's intellectual and interpretive scaffolding, its underlying concepts which we all use to arrive at judgements of value, can no longer sustain us. Perhaps it was possible for human beings, once, to buy into the idea that value has a basis in something beyond this world (say God or the Absolute), but no longer. We are on the verge of a spiritual crisis, and something new is needed to sustain us, otherwise we plummet into the horrors of nihilism or worse.

Nietzsche views this crisis with something approaching joy, because he sees in it a new kind of freedom, a freedom to find value for ourselves. His catchphrase for the crisis of value is 'God is dead', and it is easy to hear the happiness in Nietzsche's voice when you read it. Consider this passage:

> In fact, we philosophers and 'free spirits' feel ourselves irradiated as by a new dawn by the report that the 'old God is dead'; our hearts overflow with gratitude, astonishment, presentiment and expectation. At last, the horizon seems open once more, granting even that it is not bright; our ships can at last put out to sea in face of every danger; every hazard is again permitted to the discerner; the sea, *our* sea, again lies open before us; perhaps never before did such an 'open sea' exist.

Nietzsche's treatment of moral value is instructive, an illustration of what he takes to be free-thinking in the light of the realization that the current conceptions of value are bankrupt. His discussion is philosophical, though some deny this, as well as philological, quasi-historical and, at times, verging on psychoanalytical. By laying bare the alleged meaning and history of our moral values, Nietzsche hopes to undermine them, reveal them for what they really are, and replace them with something better.

It is very easy to lose one's way in all of this, owing principally to Nietzsche's style – clarity and argumentation is sometimes exchanged for rhetoric and good prose. Nietzsche calls himself an 'immoralist', suggesting that he renounces all conceptions of morality, but in fact he only wishes to reject the West's present moral categories. He also says that the admirable person is 'a creator of values', and some see in this a kind of radical relativism or egoism, the view that each individual ought merely to function according to their own notion of right and wrong, perhaps only look after their own interests. This is probably another misreading. In fact, Nietzsche is calling for us to return to the moral concepts held by the Ancient Greeks. Morality, for both Nietzsche and at least some of the Greeks, depends on human nature; in particular it is an expression of what is excellent in us. For Nietzsche, though, human nature is not universal – our natures are different, and it therefore follows that different people can find and follow different conceptions of excellence, different moralities.

Morality and the Will to Power

In saying all of this, Nietzsche makes a distinction between master-morality and slave-morality. In the former kind of morality, the nobles or ruling classes call what is best in themselves 'good' (truthfulness, power, pride in oneself) and what they despise in those they rule 'bad' (weakness, lies, timidity, insignificance). The slaves, and in particular those with a priestly impulse, see things differently. In their impotence, unable to exercise power of any sort on their masters, they invert master-morality. 'Good' is now applied to weakness, meekness, suffering and loss, as well as those qualities most needed by the weak: sympathy, humility, friendliness and patience. 'Evil' becomes a term of abuse levelled by the weak at the properties of the strong they most despise: their health, power and strength. Nietzsche writes: '... the wretched alone are the good; the poor, impotent, lowly alone are the good; the suffering, deprived, sick, ugly alone are pious, alone are blessed by God … and you, the powerful and noble, are on the contrary the evil, the cruel, the lustful, the insatiable, the godless to all eternity …'

The 'slave revolt' in morality, according to Nietzsche, has left us with a slave-morality, and in this strange historical moment of freedom, what is needed is something near a return to master-morality.

Man and Superman

The return is exemplified by the *Übermensch* (the Overman or Superman), that being which has overcome what has so far defined us as human, the now-crumbling system of value. Humanity, such as it is, is now something to be overcome, and the Overman is 'the lightning out of

Nietzsche (right) with his star pupil Paul Ree, and Lou Salome, in perhaps an ironic comment on Nietzsche's infamous remark, 'Thou goest to woman? Forget not thy whip'.

the dark cloud of man', the new ideal at which to aim. Nietzsche labels as 'human, all too human' the religious or transcendental hopes and illusions characterized by our current dying scheme of value: the belief that virtue consists in obeying the will of a dead God, that the fictitious rewards of the next life somehow excuse subjugation in this one, and so on. The Overman renounces all of this, carving out his place in the world according to his own will.

The notion of will – in particular, the will to power – determines much of Nietzsche's thinking. Some incautious remarks in some of his notebooks suggest that Nietzsche might have toyed with the thought that everything is will to power, that the will to power is the elementary force underlying all reality or the fundamental explanatory principle. It first appears in his published work as one drive among others, a striving for control, but it is clear that in the end Nietzsche thought it was much more than this. Nietzsche has his prophet, Zarathustra, asserting that all life is will to power. In later works, he calls it 'a life-affirming drive', and it is possible to settle on the view that, at the very least, the will to power is a kind of brute tendency for self-assertion manifested in us all. Couple this interpretation with his remarks on what is good, and one can begin to make some sense of otherwise perplexing passages.

But in reading Nietzsche, we want more than just sense; what we're after is truth. If what Nietzsche is proposing is a new conception of morality, then it should have some advice in it, shouldn't it? It should give us some thoughts on how to live, some idea of what we ought to value, some conception of rightness and wrongness in action. It's all very well to say that some return to the Greeks is required, that we must find our own value, but without further advice, isn't this just empty bad air?

It is difficult to think along such lines without imagining Nietzsche shaking with rage at the very thought of such an objection. His point is that human beings have had enough advice, enough listening, enough following. If we are to overcome the very herd instincts which motivate this kind of objection, we are going to have to do some thinking for ourselves.

MAJOR WORKS

The Birth of Tragedy (1872)
This recasts Greek culture in terms of wild Dionysian energy, rather than sober Apollonian reserve. Nietzsche sees in such energy the possibility of creative, cultural and spiritual rebirth.

Human, All-Too-Human (1878)
A collection of usually pithy but sometimes perplexing aphorisms on an enormous range of topics. Here, the notion of power makes a genuine appearance in Nietzsche's writings.

Thus Spoke Zarathustra (1883–85)
A work among Nietzsche's most important writings. It recounts the development of Zarathustra, who prophesizes the coming of the Overman and what might lie beyond the human condition.

Beyond Good and Evil (1886)
Nietzsche's account of morality which also contains a mature expression of the will to power.

The Genealogy of Morals (1887)
It is possible to read this as a critique of Christian morality. It includes Nietzsche's account of the 'slave revolt' in morality, as well as a blistering critique of the priesthood. It concludes with an expression of perspectivalism.

Edmund Husserl

Edmund Husserl (1859–1938) was the originator of the philosophy of phenomenology, which would come into its own during the twentieth century.

HUSSERL'S LIKING FOR NEW WORDS, and new uses for old words, makes him a difficult philosopher to read. In the eyes of Husserl scholars, this is almost certainly thought to be a good thing, for they like nothing better than to entertain each other with talk of epochés, eidic reduction, noemata, horizons and hyle. Normally, there would be little excuse for this kind of thing, but, in the case of Husserl, we can perhaps forgive him the technical vocabulary, for he did invent a new philosophical approach, one which dominated much of philosophy in the continental tradition in the twentieth century.

He called this approach 'phenomenology', which, in its most general sense, consists of the analysis and explication of the structures of conscious experience. Husserl's interest in consciousness can be traced to his formative years and the influence of his teachers.

He was born in Prossnitz, Moravia, then a part of the Austrian Empire, and now in the Czech Republic, on 8 April 1859. When he was 10, his father, a clothing merchant, sent him to Vienna to begin his education proper at the Realgymnasium. Shortly afterwards, he moved a lot closer to home when he transferred to the public gymnasium in Olmütz. Although he did not excel at school, he nevertheless developed a passion for science and mathematics. He graduated in 1876 and then went on to study physics, mathematics, astronomy and philosophy at the universities of Leipzig, Berlin and Vienna. He received his doctorate in 1882, with a dissertation titled 'Contributions to the Theory of the Calculus of Variations'. Then he made what was perhaps the decisive move of his intellectual life when he went to Vienna to study with the German philosopher and psychologist Franz Brentano in 1884.

Brentano's importance lies primarily in the fact that he developed the concept of intentionality, which is central to phenomenology. Intentionality refers to the directedness of consciousness; consciousness is always consciousness *of* something. Brentano famously put it like this:

> Every mental phenomenon is characterised by what the Scholastics of the Middle Ages called the intentional (or mental) inexistence of an object, and what we might call, though not wholly unambiguously, reference to a con-

tent, direction toward an object … Every mental phenomenon includes something as object within itself, although they do not do so in the same way. In presentation, something is presented, in judgement something is affirmed or denied, in love loved, in hate hated, in desire desired and so on. (*Psychology from an Empirical Standpoint*)

Husserl, in his turn, expressed it thus:

The terminological expression … for designating the basic character of being as consciousness, as consciousness of something, is intentionality. In the unreflective holding of some object or other in consciousness, we are turned or directed towards it: our 'intentio' goes out towards it. (*Introduction to Phenomenology*)

This basic idea is fairly easy to understand: consciousness, in its various aspects, is always directed towards an object. Thus, for example, a person might perceive a dog; desire an ice-cream; judge a contest; remember a birthday party; or contemplate a sunset. However, in its details, it rapidly becomes much more complicated. For example, consider the case of hallucination: if a person thinks that they see a unicorn, given that consciousness is necessarily directed towards an object, is the unicorn then in some sense real? Brentano's response – though it is still a matter of scholarly debate, and it is an issue about which he never reached a settled opinion – was that the object has a kind of existence within the realm of the mental. Husserl disagreed: he argued that consciousness is merely *as if of* an object; the existence, or not, of the objects of consciousness is a secondary matter.

Rorschach ink blot. Just as what we see in the blot depends on who we are, how we perceive the external world, says Husserl, will be shaped by our experiences, our interests, our entire consciousness.

Phenomenological Reduction

The best way to get an idea of what Husserl had in mind here is to consider his notion of 'phenomenological reduction'. This is perhaps the central phenomenological technique. It comprises a special way of attending to the objects which appear to consciousness. Rather than treating them as everyday objects – for example, the next door neighbour's dog with the red collar – about which we already have ideas and theories, we treat them simply as appearances. We put their existence in 'brackets', suspend our 'natural attitude' towards them, in order to consider them purely as they appear to consciousness; we remain neutral on the question of their existence.

Husserl hoped that by focusing on pure experience in this way it would be possible to learn something about the structure which constitutes the directedness of consciousness. However, this emphasis on the subjective elements of experience has led to the accusation that Husserl is some kind of philosophical idealist, that is, that he does not believe that the world has a reality which is independent of our experience of it. It is easy to see how people have come to this conclusion. Indeed, Husserl himself termed his approach transcendental idealism; and, moreover, he argued that consciousness constitutes its objects. Yet, at the same time, he claimed that it was indubitable that the world exists.

At first sight this might seem paradoxical, and certainly many commentators do find it so. Indeed, one of the major criticisms of Husserl's approach is that he gets stuck in the realm of appearances; that, like **Descartes**, he has no easy way to move from the subjective into the objective. There is a certain irony in this because his wider project was aimed at establishing an objective foundation for all knowledge. He had been impressed with Descartes's method of radical doubt, but felt it was not carried far enough; hence his insistence that in phenomenological reduction it is necessary to 'bracket' all that we think we know about the world. However, the result is this tension between the subjective and the objective.

Consciousness and the External World

Despite this, there is at least the beginnings of a way out from what seems to be the paradox of claiming that consciousness constitutes the objects to which it is directed and yet also that the external world has a reality of its own. Husserl's position appears to be that what comes in from the outside is not sufficient to determine our consciousness of it. To understand how this might be, consider, for example, what happens when we look out onto a street on a foggy night. We will see shapes, yet precisely how these shapes appear to each one of us will vary according to our previous experiences, interests, cultural identity, and so on. To give a very simple example, a person who has spent all their life in the Amazon jungle will see different things in the street than the person who has always lived in cities. Consciousness in this way, then, structures what we see; it is constitutive of our experience of the external world.

Husserl has been accused of being a philosophical idealist, of denying the reality of the world external to our consciousness.

The Influence of Phenomenology

Phenomenology has been hugely influential. In the world of philosophy, it underpins the work of such thinkers as **Heidegger**, **Sartre** and Merleau-Ponty. Thus, for example, Heidegger dedicated his great work *Being and Time* to Husserl (though he later withdrew the dedication); and Sartre, in *Being and Nothingness*, stated that 'all consciousness, as Husserl has shown, is consciousness of something', and he used this insight as the foundation upon which to build his existential theory of human freedom.

Phenomenology has also been influential beyond the world of philosophy. For instance, in the social sciences, Husserl's concept of the *lifeworld*, the taken-for-granted world of our everyday lives, has received much attention. The sociologist Alfred Schutz, for example, spent a good part of his intellectual life explicating the structures of the lifeworld as they are both constituted and experienced by human beings. Thus, in his book *The Phenomenology of the Social World*, he argued that we experience the lifeworld as our natural world, one that we take for granted and gear into in the pursuit of our projects and life-plans. Consequently, it requires something akin to a shock for us to break out of the bounds of this world to enter the realm of another world. According to Schutz, however, such shocks occur frequently in the course of our lives. He mentions, as examples, the shock of falling to sleep as the transition into the realm of dreams; the Kierkegaardian 'leap' into the world of religious experience; and the transformation that occurs as the curtain rises in a theatre.

It is hard to draw definitive conclusions about Husserl's significance as a philosopher. Whilst it is true that the high point of phenomenology is now in the past, he remains a major figure in the continental tradition of philosophy. Moreover, a number of analytic philosophers, particularly those working in the philosophy of mind, have begun to take his work seriously. However, it is likely that he will always remain a slightly marginal figure in the pantheon of greats. There are a couple of reasons for this. First, his style of writing; it is fair to say that it is is not good, and it is undoubtedly a barrier to a greater appreciation of his work. Second, the fact that he did not complete the philosophical task which he set himself; in the end, his aim of establishing the firm foundations for all human knowledge went unfulfilled.

The last few years of his life were both eventful and difficult. The rise of Nazism led to him being denied the use of the library at the University of Freiburg, where he had taught until 1928, and to him being excluded generally from German academic life. He nevertheless continued to work, bolstered by the daily walks he took with his friend and research assistant Eugen Fink, visits from philosophical colleagues, and invitations to lecture abroad. In 1937, he became ill, and by the beginning of 1938 it was clear that he would not live much longer. But he remained a philosopher to the end. At his death, he refused spiritual counselling, saying that he had lived as a philosopher and wanted to die as one.

MAJOR WORKS

Logical Investigations (1900-1901)
This work is made up of two volumes: the first is a criticism of 'psychologism' in the study of logic; the second, an analysis of the key themes of the phenomenological method. These studies are generally considered to be Husserl's first in the area of phenomenology.

Ideas (3 volumes 1913)
Very difficult exposition of the major themes of phenomenology. Introduces, and/or develops, many of the major concepts associated with Husserl's approach, including intentionality, transcendental reduction, noema, noesis and hyle.

Formal and Transcendental Logic (1929)
As the title suggests, this book deals with the phenomenological foundations of formal logic. As with *Ideas*, it is a very difficult text for people not familiar with Husserl to get to grips with.

Cartesian Meditations (1931)
Perhaps the easiest of Husserl's later works, it is a reworking and expansion of a series of lectures which were given at the Sorbonne in 1929. Its focus is primarily the phenomenology of the ego, and the processes which underpin and constitute intersubjectivity.

Crisis of European Sciences and Transcendental Phenomenology (1936)
In this work, there is a move away from the more abstract concerns of the earlier works towards instead a concern with the lifeworld. This book is amongst the most influential of Husserl's, particularly in that it played an important role in extending phenomenology into the social sciences.

John Dewey

As well as a psychologist and progressive educational reformer, John Dewey (1859–1952) was one of the more influential American philosophers of the last century. With Peirce and James, he is associated with the pragmatic school of philosophy.

As a graduate student of psychology, Dewey became impressed with the scientific method.

JOHN DEWEY (1859–1952) WAS BORN IN BURLINGTON, Vermont, USA, on 20 October 1859, the third of the four sons of Archibald Dewey and Lucina Rich. He was brought up in modest circumstances. His father, a grocer, made a comfortable living, but was not particularly ambitious on the behalf of his children; though he had a passion for Shakespeare and Milton and was in the habit of reciting Burns to his sons. He would have been quite content for them to have become tradesmen. Dewey's mother, 20 years younger than her husband, was, however, of different character; more intense and ambitious, and it was mainly at her urging that the three surviving boys – the eldest sibling having died in infancy – pursued college educations at the University of Vermont.

It was as an undergraduate that the seeds of Dewey's later intellectual commitments were first sown. Particularly, it was at this time that he came into contact with evolutionary thought, and the lessons he learnt were to stay with him for the rest of his life. In the pre-modern world, species and organisms were seen as immutable, perfectly defined entities, the product of a benevolent designer. Darwin's theory blew this idea apart, showing that the natural world is in fact dynamic and fluid, and that organisms and species are ever-changing as they interact with their environment. This idea of iterative change became central to Dewey's conception of human nature. He rejected the idea that humans have a fundamental essence, and all that this involves in terms of the ends towards which their lives are directed, and the means employed to attain these ends, arguing instead that human beings are constituted in their interaction with the multiple aspects of their environment. Humans are through and through the product of a lived practice.

It wasn't only in the area of evolutionary thought that Dewey came to see the importance of a scientific way of thinking. As a graduate student at Johns Hopkins University, he came into contact with G. Stanley Hall, an experimental psychologist of international repute. Dewey was impressed with the power of the scientific method, and in his early writings he sought to reconcile it with Hegelian idealism. This, however, was not successful, and by the early 1890s, after he had taken up a position at the University of Chicago, he abandoned his idealism for the empirical, instrumental approach that he espoused for the next 60 years.

Dewey (centre) espouses the creation of a liberal third party in US politics at a convention of the League for Independent Political Action, 1932.

The Theory of Inquiry

At the centre of this approach is his theory of inquiry, which aimed to show how thought emerges as people interact with their environments, and how the measure of true belief – or belief for which there is warranted assertability – is that it facilitates satisfactory responses to the circumstances which people confront, or, to put this another way, that it provides successful rules for conduct.

The best way of understanding this idea is first to consider what Dewey meant by the notion of 'habit'. As we have seen, he did not think that humans have a fixed, determinate nature. However, it is nevertheless the case that people tend to behave in fairly predictable ways. This is because they have learnt, via the process of socialization, particular socially sanctioned habits. It is in this fashion that people are able to get by in their lives; they have adopted the modes of behaviour which function to achieve specific goals in particular circumstances.

However, sometimes these habits break down; the actions and responses people can draw upon prove inadequate in terms of the situations they confront, and they cannot go on. It is at this point there appears the kind of genuine doubt which necessitates inquiry. In *How We Think* Dewey emphasized that this sort of doubt is not purely cognitive, not the doubt of a sceptical philosopher, it is *felt* doubt:

> In cases of striking novelty or unusual perplexity, the difficulty … is likely to present itself at first as a shock, as emotional disturbance, as a more or less vague feeling of the unexpected, of something queer, strange, funny, or disconcerting. In such instances, there are necessary observations deliberately calculated to bring to light just what is the trouble, or to make clear the specific character of the problem.

Having identified that there is a difficulty which needs addressing, in order to avoid the fairly ad hoc construction of possible solutions, the next stage in the process of inquiry is to isolate the significant elements of the problematic situation. Once this is achieved, then it is necessary to determine a number of hypotheses in order to solve the difficulty. This is a creative, imaginative process, and it involves going beyond what is given in the situation: '… it is more or less speculative, adventurous … it involves a leap, a jump, the propriety of which cannot be absolutely warranted in advance, no matter what precautions be taken' (*How We Think*).

John Dewey

The final stages in the process involve working through the implications of the various hypotheses which are being entertained, and then, crucially, testing them experimentally:

> Reasoning shows that if the idea be adopted, certain consequences follow. So far the conclusion is hypothetical or conditional. If we look and find present all the conditions demanded by the theory, and if we find the characteristic traits called for by rival alternatives to be lacking, the tendency to believe, to accept, is almost irresistible. (*How We Think*)

The resolution of this process involves the incorporation of new beliefs into the framework of habits which allows people to act in concert with the events in their lives. Truth is that which works. For Dewey, then, it is a mistake to think, following **Descartes**, that the fundamental epistemological question is to do with how we can know that the stuff in our minds, our perceptions, corresponds with external reality. Rather, what counts is whether our beliefs provide us with rules of conduct which help us to interact with the world.

There is an important point here about the status of true beliefs, or, to adopt Dewey's terminology, 'warranted assertions'. Like **Peirce**, Dewey is committed to a fallibilistic epistemology. Beliefs constitute knowledge when they are confirmed by a community of genuine enquirers. However, the extent of the warrant varies, and all beliefs are subject to revision, not least because the circumstances in which problematic situations arise are changed by the very act of finding solutions to them.

Dewey extends his theory of inquiry into the moral domain. Just as he denied that there was an inviolate human essence, so he denied that there were absolute moral standards – whether they be handed down by religious or philosophic

MAJOR WORKS

How We Think (1910)
This early work outlines Dewey's theory of inquiry; and suggests that beliefs will be adopted or rejected on the basis of their usefulness in allowing people to master the situations which they confront in their lives.

Democracy and Education (1916)
It represents the most systematic articulation of Dewey's ideas about education, stressing the importance of active, cooperative learning, and denying that education should be seen merely as preparation for civic and economic responsibilities. Also provides an interesting introduction to Dewey's more general philosophical ideas.

Human Nature and Conduct (1922)
This book seeks to establish a moral theory based on the study of human nature. Although this will not solve all moral problems, it is argued that it will allow them to be posed in such a way that it might be possible to work towards solving them.

The Public and Its Problems (1927)
This defends the ideal of participatory democracy against critics who had argued that the nature of modern societies precludes anything more than a severely restricted kind of democracy.

Logic: The Theory of Inquiry (1938)
Major statement of Dewey's pragmatism, and the theory of inquiry which underpins it.

authority – which remain true even in changing circumstances. The goal of moral action then is not to conform to a given code of behaviour, which would function merely to limit the expression of human potentiality, but rather to approach every situation with a view to constructing it in such a way that it offers the best opportunities for human fulfilment.

Value Judgements

This point can be illustrated by considering how value judgements work. For Dewey, value judgements are practical judgements; they guide the behaviour we exhibit towards the things which we value (our 'valuings'). Value judgements come into play when our normal activity towards our valuings has been disrupted by a problematic situation – for example, I have found that I cannot get to sleep if I drink coffee late at night. The point of the value judgement – I ought to drink warm milk instead – is to enable one to adopt a new course of action, if required, in order to solve the problematic situation. Thus, value judgements are tools which function to help us to live better lives.

It is only possible to engage in this kind of moral reasoning if we cultivate the same habits of inquiry which are appropriate for finding out new things about the world. The measure of the appropriateness of a value judgement is how well it works in the world; that is, whether it results in consequences which we value as we hypothesized that we would – did I, in fact, sleep better having drunk warm milk rather than coffee before bed? Value judgements, then, like the judgements we make about things in the world, are subject to empirical verification. They are also necessarily provisional and revisable in the face of changing circumstances.

To accomplish scientific and moral reasoning in line with the precepts of Dewey's theory of inquiry requires that individuals are capable of flexible and sophisticated thought. There are clear implications here for the way that people should be educated. Particularly, Dewey argued that education should not be overly didactic in form; the idea is not simply to impart information which students will passively absorb. Rather, proper education aims to foster imaginative responses to new information and situations by engaging students in active, cooperative practices of learning. In this way, people develop the skills and habits required to enable them to function happily as full members of communities founded on principles of democratic participation.

John Dewey officially retired in 1930, but continued to teach as Professor Emeritus at the University of Columbia, where he had been working since 1904, until 1939. By this time, he was the pre-eminent figure in American philosophy. Even after he finished teaching, this was not the end of his philosophical and public activities. Most notably, he was the chairperson of the Commission of Inquiry which, on investigating the charges made against Leon Trotsky in the Moscow trials of the mid-1930s, found in favour of Trotsky and against Stalin.

Dewey died in 1952 at the age of 92. By this time, pragmatism was attracting less interest from professional philosophers. However, Dewey's place as a major figure in the philosophical firmament is assured. His criticisms of the classical tradition in Western philosophy remain pertinent today. He is a major influence in liberal, progressive thought. And moreover, there are today signs of a revival of interest in his ideas, particularly in the work of people like Richard Rorty and Jürgen Habermas.

Bertrand Russell

Generally recognized as one of the founders of analytical philosophy, Bertrand Russell (1872–1970) is perhaps Britain's best-known, and most controversial, philosophical commentator of modern times.

REFLECTION ON THE LIFE OF BERTRAND RUSSELL, Third Earl Russell, can be a little tiring. He seems to have crammed a lot of living into a life that was unusually long. He probably did more than anyone in the first decades of the twentieth century to put philosophy on the course of logical analysis it generally still holds today. It equipped him with a method, and using it he came to large conclusions in the philosophy of mathematics, metaphysics and epistemology. Without doubt, he was a brilliant mathematician, and according to some sources his insights into set theory had more than a little to do with the development of computing.

You might conclude from this that Russell was a wild-haired, desiccated calculating machine, detached from practical matters, but you would be quite wrong. Not only was he presentable and socially graceful, but he was an excellent stylist – he won the Nobel Prize for Literature in 1950 – and his many public writings, particularly his *History of Western Philosophy* and *The Problems of Philosophy*, more often than not manage the rare combination of rigour and readability. He was also a very public figure, campaigning for civil rights and protesting against war and nuclear weapons, spending time in prison for his efforts. The story of his private life is a little darker and perhaps less admirable.

Russell was born in Trelleck, Monmouthshire, Wales, to Lord Amberley, oldest son of the First Earl Russell, and Kate Stanley, daughter of the second Baron Stanley of Alderly. His parents were dead by the time Russell was four years old, and this seems unusually tragic, both because he was then raised a little sternly by his austere, Unitarian grandmother and because Russell, by temperament, would have got on spectacularly well with his parents. He did not actually come to know much about them until he was 18, and it was probably with some delight that he discovered, as he writes with unconcealed pride in the first sentence of 'My Religious Reminiscences', that they were 'considered shocking in their day on account of their advanced opinions in politics, theology and morals'.

Lord Amberley, for example, got himself thrown out of Parliament when it was discovered that he supported the use of birth control. Lady Amberley, for her part, spoke publicly in defence of women's suffrage, somehow managing to annoy Queen Victoria, who allegedly fumed, 'I

Along with GE Moore, Russell led the revolt against 'British Idealism' grounding his arguments in logic & mathematics.

wish I could whip that Kate Amberley.' The Amberleys were long-standing admir-
ers of Bentham and Mill, and eventually became friends with the latter,
contemplating the possibility of asking Mill to be the secular equivalent of Russell's
godfather. Given his parent's early death, it is hard not to wonder what sort of
philosopher Russell might have become had things turned out differently. A young
Russell tutored at Mill's knee is an image it is difficult to clear from one's mind.

Russell took a place at Trinity College, Cambridge, to study mathematics, eventually turning to philosophy. He was appointed lecturer at Trinity, but his loud and
public opposition to the First World War led to his dismissal and, eventually, a
prison term. He was reappointed but finally resigned from Trinity, becoming
dependent on popular writings for an income. He remained politically active
throughout his life, well into his nineties, campaigning against America's involvement in Vietnam and serving as a vocal proponent of the Campaign for Nuclear
Disarmament.

His life was also marked by a number of turbulent marriages and disastrous love
affairs, suggesting that Russell's capacity for clear-headed thinking somehow
deserted him in private life. His allegedly stunted capacity for emotion, which does
not quite square with the occasional fervour of his public campaigns, is taken as
the fundamental explanatory principle required for an understanding of Russell's
personality by some biographers. It is hard to know just what to think in this connection.

The Revolt against Idealism

When Russell came of age at Trinity, the final stages of an intellectual shift in British
philosophy from empiricism to variations on the idealisms of **Kant** and **Hegel** were
being articulated by F.H. Bradley. In *Appearance and Reality*, Bradley operates with
a modification of the Kantian distinction between the mind-constituted world of
appearances and the world as it is in itself. The distinction is roughly between prop-
ertied objects standing in causal relations to one another in space and time on the
one hand and reality itself on the other, which Bradley takes to be something akin
to the Hegelian Absolute, a single Cosmic Experience of which we are a small, self-
conscious part. Odd tenets follow from the view. For example, the very idea of
independently existing things (bacon sandwiches and plates) standing in relations
to one another (the bacon sandwich is on the plate) is incoherent. Reality itself is
unified, and the appearance of distinct objects, as well as relations between them,
is illusory. 'Truths' about particulars, on this view, can only be partial.

Along with G.E. Moore, Russell led the revolt against British Idealism. While
Moore deployed arguments rooted in common sense and ordinary language,
Russell's arguments were grounded in logic and mathematics, the so-called 'logi-
cal-analytic method'. By expanding the scope of logic dramatically, along with
A.N. Whitehead in the monumental *Principia Mathematica*, Russell shows that it is
possible to restate propositions in a more rigorous and revealing logical form. This
can sometimes uncover errors – such as vagueness, equivocation, or other sorts of
confusions – in our everyday and philosophical talk. In addition to this and in
direct reply to the idealists, Russell hoped to find a way to make talk of concrete
particular objects, their properties and relations, logically respectable and clear,
showing up confusions in idealist arguments in the process. The result was devas-

Bertrand Russell

tating to idealism, which more or less died the death in the English-speaking world, and it put logical analysis at the centre of twentieth-century philosophizing.

Although Russell's various positions changed throughout his life – he made no apology for this, claiming that mental stagnation was far worse than the occasional revision of philosophical doctrine – he applied the same method to virtually all of the largest philosophical questions going. It might be that the method is more important than the answers he gives. He characterizes his view of the process in this passage:

> It seems to me that philosophical investigation, as far as I have experience of it, starts from that curious and unsatisfactory state of mind in which one feels complete certainty without being able to say what one is certain of. The process that results from prolonged attention is just like that of watching an object approaching through a thick fog … It seems to me that those who object to analysis would wish us to be content with the initial dark blur.

Even if we place a higher value on Russell's method than the content of his thinking, this is to take nothing away from that content. There is no question that the content has had large implications for the philosophy of mathematics, epistemology and metaphysics.

The Problem of the External World

Consider Russell's response to the problem of how we know the nature of objects in the external world. Russell begins with reflections on perceptual experience. We seem to see tables, chairs and books in the room, but closer inspection reveals that we are not quite seeing what we normally take ourselves to see. We suppose, for example, that the table is brown, perhaps uniformly brown, brown all over. However, parts of the table reflect light differently, and if you move your head around you will notice that the reflective parts shift around too. The apparent shape of the table changes as well – from above it looks circular, but from the side it looks elliptical. Putting other heads, other points of view, into the equation complicates

MAJOR WORKS

Principia Mathematica (with A N Whitehead) (1910–13)
A massive, three volume explication of Russell's theory of mathematics. It contains his important theory of types, as well as a defence of logicism, the view that mathematics is a part of logic.

The Problems of Philosophy (1912)
Still among the very best popular or introductory books of philosophy, this slim volume manages to combine philosophical integrity with a clear, readable style.

A History of Western Philosophy (1945)
This is probably Russell's best known work. It is a masterful treatment, a clear explication of the whole of Western Philosophy.

Bertrand Russell: Logic and Knowledge (1965)
A collection of some of Russell's most important essays. It contains his 'Lectures on the Philosophy of Logical Atomism', the view that the world is made up of logical atoms – fleeting patches of colour or snippets of sounds, predicates, relations and the facts composed of these atoms.

matters further. What then are we seeing when we claim to see a table? What's the real table? '… [T]he real table, if there is one, is not the same as what we immediately experience by sight or touch or hearing. The real table, if there is one, is not *immediately* known to us at all, but must be an inference from what is immediately known.'

Russell calls the ever-shifting appearances 'sense-data'. It is sense-data which we immediately know, with which we are directly acquainted, and about which it is hard to think we might be wrong. What is needed is a connection between sense-data and objects, and here Russell admits that the view of objects as substances cannot stand. A new conception of objects as logical constructions built out of or inferred from sense-data is required. On at least one reading of Russell's view (and Russell's account changed over time), objects are sets or collections of perspectives. It is important to notice that this is saying something different and something less than that we infer the existence of an object (in the usual sense) on the basis of sense-data. Instead, Russell is claiming that the objects themselves are logical constructions, not substances out there causing sense-data, at least not in a straightforward sense.

You can wonder, maybe unkindly, what these constructions of perspectives are perspectives on, and in so wondering you might have made a syntactical error which a good student of logic might be able to clear up for you. You can also take it that Russell's claims, to have any meat on the bones at all, have to be a form of inferential realism, the view that the existence of objects, even logically constructed objects, is somehow inferred from sense-data. If this is the right interpretation, you can object in the same way everyone objects to this sort of view: it seems to make the table invisible, and that can't be right.

There is another, more general objection to Russell's views and method, an objection he considered himself. All of this seems to make philosophy a branch of science or logic, seems to rob philosophy of what is most attractive about it, the speculative freedom or playfulness attending philosophical reflection. Reducing philosophical problems to complex, dry logical or mathematical matters makes the world boring. If this is true, Russell says:

> … then it's not my fault, and therefore I do not feel I owe any apology for any sort of dryness or dullness in the world. I would say this too, that for those who have any taste for mathematics, for those who like symbolic constructions, that sort of world is a very delightful one, and if you do not find it otherwise attractive, all that is necessary to do is to acquire a taste for mathematics, and then you will have a very agreeable world …

Many philosophers since Russell have taken this advice, a few going much further than Russell in circumscribing the limits of philosophical reflection to a more narrow range than even Russell would have liked. Still, the philosophical world as it is, no doubt because of the emphasis on logic in Russell's writings, would be a very agreeable world to him.

Russell was nothing if not a passionate, committed philosopher. Here he addresses a crowd in Trafalgar Square at an anti-nuclear weapons rally.

Ludwig Wittgenstein

Many people believe that Ludwig Wittgenstein (1889–1951) was the twentieth century's most important philosopher. It is somewhat ironic, then, that he is probably best known for waving a poker at fellow philosopher Karl Popper.

1889–1951

THE SETTING FOR THIS PECULIAR EVENT WAS A MEETING of the Cambridge Moral Science Club in October 1946. There are different accounts of precisely what took place, but the general gist of it is that in the midst of a heated discussion about the validity of moral rules, Wittgenstein picked up a poker, gesticulated with it in order to make a point, and then abruptly departed the scene. Popper is said to have subsequently given as an example of a moral rule that one should not threaten visiting lecturers with pokers.

Wittgenstein's biographers all agree, as this story suggests, that he was an intense, if compelling, personality. He was born in Vienna on 20 April 1889, the youngest child of Leopoldine and Karl Wittgenstein. His father was a rich and successful Austrian industrialist and enjoyed a position of some prominence in Viennese society. The Wittgenstein home was a centre of cultural excellence; Brahms and Mahler were frequent visitors, and the young Wittgenstein was encouraged in these early years, particularly by his mother, to develop his own musical interests.

His formal education, however, was a little unorthodox. He did not attend school until he was 14, and then not very successfully. It was assumed that like his father he would become an engineer – indeed, he had shown some aptitude in this direction – so, having failed in his ambition to read physics at university, he went off to study engineering, first in Berlin and then in Manchester. It was whilst at Manchester that he became interested in philosophy; he had read and been impressed by Bertrand **Russell**'s *Principles of Mathematics*, and on the advice of Frege, with whom he had corresponded, he went to Cambridge in 1912 to study with Russell.

The Picture Theory of Meaning

Although it was immediately clear that he was a brilliant thinker, he only stayed in Cambridge for a short while, opting instead to travel. However, this was interrupted in 1914 by the start of the First World War. Wittgenstein immediately joined the Austrian army, serving mainly on the eastern front. During this time, he worked on the manuscript of the book which would eventually become *Tractatus Logico-Philosophicus*, his first great work.

The *Tractatus* was eventually published in 1922 with the help of Russell. It is a short book, only seventy pages long, but Wittgenstein, for a while at least, seemed to believe that it solved all the genuine problems of philosophy. The book set out what is known as the picture theory of meaning. The world is constituted by a set of atomic facts. Propositions – for example, the cat is black – are logical pictures of actual or possible facts; in other words, propositions stand for possible states of affair of the world. If the state of affair picked out by a proposition obtains in the world, then the proposition is true. Thus, it was Wittgenstein's claim that the underlying logical structure of language mirrors the logical structure of the world.

It must be said that it is hard to be clear about Wittgenstein's argument unless one has a thorough grounding in the issues which informed the work on language and logic of people like Frege, Russell and Whitehead. However, there is an interesting general point about Wittgenstein's argument in the *Tractatus*. It was his view that language allows things to be said clearly or not at all: 'What can be said at all can be said clearly, and what we cannot talk about we must pass over in silence.'

Moreover, language marks the limits of thought; therefore, if it isn't possible to say something clearly, it isn't possible to think it without falling into nonsense. Part of the significance of this argument is that it led Wittgenstein to the thought that philosophy is a highly circumscribed endeavour. It is mainly about policing the limits of language; ensuring that that we don't fall into the error of mistaking nonsense for meaning. Indeed, Wittgenstein famously said at the end of the *Tractatus*: 'My propositions serve as elucidations in the following way: anyone who understands me eventually recognises them as nonsensical.'

Nonsensical or not, Wittgenstein took his cue from the publication of the *Tractatus* to give up philosophy for a while. He disappeared to Austria, where he took a job as a schoolteacher. This was not an entirely successful endeavour. There were accusations of almost tyrannical teaching practices – including an alleged incident of violence towards a female student (though there were no reports that a poker was used!) – and eventually he gave up teaching to become a gardener at a monastery. At this point, something interesting happened. Wittgenstein began to talk with some of the members of the Vienna circle group of philosophers, in particular, with Moritz Schlick, and he came to the view that perhaps the *Tractatus* had not solved all the genuine philosophical problems after all.

This reassessment led to the second phase of Wittgenstein's philosophical career, in which he developed ideas which in many respects were completely at odds with his earlier philosophy. In particular, he came to believe that the idea that language is a determinate system, within which simple propositions stand for states of affairs of the world, was fundamentally misconceived. Rather, language is multifaceted and context-dependent; it is used for and accomplishes many different things. Thus, for example, it simply isn't possible to say how the phrase 'I love you, too' will be understood unless the context in which it is said is known. To say it in response to an insult is to intend something entirely different than if it is said to a lover in a tender moment. Meaning is inextricably tied to the behaviour of language users and the contexts in which they employ speech acts.

Philosophical Investigations
These new ideas about language and meaning were articulated most significantly

in the posthumously published *Philosophical Investigations*. In this work, Wittgenstein set out to show that language gains its meaning from the way in which it is used: 'For a *large* class of cases – though not for all – in which we employ the word "meaning" it can be defined thus: the meaning of a word is its use in the language.'

Linked to this idea is the notion of a 'language-game'; the ways and contexts in which words are used depends upon the 'game' being played. The idea of the language-game brings into focus the fact that language is linked to specific activities, or particular 'forms of life'. Wittgenstein mentioned as examples the following: giving orders and obeying them; reporting an event; speculating about an event; putting together a hypothesis; joke-telling; cursing and story-telling. Much of *Investigations* is concerned with flagging the differences within and between various language games.

A Private Language

Perhaps the most talked about section of *Investigations* is where Wittgenstein argued against the possibility of a private language. The argument is not presented in a standard way, with premises, deduction and conclusions. Rather, in line with the style of the book as a whole, it is constructed out of a series of short statements, with little explication of their meaning and intent. Consequently, there are many different interpretations of the private language argument; what follows, therefore, is just one particular interpretation.

Wittgenstein asks whether it is possible to 'imagine a language in which a person could write down or give vocal expression to his inner experiences – 'his feelings, moods, and the rest, where the 'individual words of this language are to refer to what can only be known to the person speaking… So another person cannot understand the language.'

To consider this possibility, he imagines the case where a person writes down 'S' in a diary every time they experience a certain sensation. In this way, it seems possible to arrive at an ostensive private definition of 'S'; every time the sensation occurs, and only when it occurs, the sign 'S' is reproduced in thought or writing, thus establishing a permanent connection between 'S' and the sensation, and thereby the meaning of the sign.

However, Wittgenstein identifies a problem with this argument. It isn't clear that we can ever establish the link between the sign 'S' and the sensation in such a way so that on those occa-

Wittgenstein in New York. From a series of screenprints based on the Wittgenstein's life and writings by Eduardo Paolozzi.

sions in the future where we employ the sign, we can be confident that we're using it correctly. In other words, in a private language there is no clear difference between remembering the correct application of a sign, and *believing* that one has remembered the correct application of a sign. As a result, the sign lacks meaning; nothing can ever establish that it is being used correctly. It follows, therefore, that a private language which refers to sensations is not possible; words gain their meaning from their use in a public context.

Although in his later work, Wittgenstein largely came to reject the arguments that he had put forward in the *Tractatus*, it would be wrong to suppose that the discontinuity between his early and later periods was total. In particular, his view of the nature of philosophy remained constant. It was Wittgenstein's belief that the task of philosophy is to uncover and analyse the various ways in which we are befuddled and confused by language. As he put it in *Investigations*, philosophy 'is a battle against the bewitchment of our intelligence by means of language'.

Wittgenstein is one of the most interesting of the great philosophers. His work, of course, has been tremendously influential. It was, for example, directly implicated in the emergence of 'ordinary language philosophy' after the Second World War. He is also interesting for reasons which are not directly to do with his philosophical output. His force of personality, for example, is renowned. He was a demanding, dramatic and intense teacher. Many of the people who attended his seminars at Trinity College were afterwards unable to imagine philosophy being conducted in any other way. He was also exceptional in the sense that he was *not* a scholar; he knew little of the standard texts of the philosophical canon, and indeed, he encouraged his students not to bother reading them. Yet he produced two distinct corpora of work, both of which would have been sufficient to establish his reputation as a great philosopher. It is quite easy to understand, then, how it is that Bertrand Russell came to consider him to be perhaps the greatest intellect of his day.

For a large class of cases...the meaning of a word is its use in the language

MAJOR WORKS

Tractatus-Logico Philosophicus (1922)
The major work of Wittgenstein's early period, and a classic of twentieth century philosophy. Outlines a picture theory of meaning, according to which meaningful propositions stand for particular states of affair of the world. A very short (20,000 words), yet hugely influential work, it was inspired by the writings of Frege, Russell and Whitehead.

Philosophical Investigations (1953)
The most important work of Wittgenstein's later period, it represents a systematic expression of the ideas which he came to hold about language and meaning. It includes an analysis of concepts such as 'language game' and 'forms of life', and pursues the idea that words gain their meaning from the rules which govern their usage.

The Blue and the Brown Books (1958)
Although posthumously published, these books originate from the mid-1930s. They were dictated by Wittgenstein to his students, and constitute a useful introduction to the ideas of his later period.

On Certainty (1969)
A collection of writings on epistemology – knowledge and certainty – from the last few years of Wittgenstein's life. Primarily sourced from his notebooks.

Martin Heidegger

It was in the nature of nineteenth-century German philosophers to tackle the big questions, of God, time, and being, head on. Martin Heidegger (1889–1976) was one of the more successful.

1889–1976

A FALLACY IS AN ERROR OF REASONING. Perhaps the most common one is the fallacy of *argumentum ad hominem* (argument to the man). An *ad hominem* is an argument directed not at the truth of a person's premises or the quality of their reasoning, but at the person themselves. It nearly goes without saying that a perfect villain can produce a fine piece of argumentation. A thug can say something true. Pointing out that a person is a villain does nothing to undercut the truth of their conclusions. Let us try to keep this logic primer firmly in mind throughout this consideration of the philosophy of Martin Heidegger. Some won't find this easy.

Heidegger was born in a small village in the Black Forest region of Germany, the eldest of the two sons of Friedrich and Johanna Heidegger. He had a religious impulse and tried to become a Jesuit but was refused on the grounds of ill health.

He took up the study of theology, physics, mathematics and philosophy at the University of Freiburg, where he came under the influence of the writings of **Husserl**. His studies were interrupted by the First World War and brief service in the army. He was discharged within a year despite swift promotion, again for health reasons. He earned his doctorate with a thesis on the relation between psychology and philosophy, eventually working as a lecturer in philosophy at Freiburg, receiving modest payment for teaching from tuition fees.

Heidegger's project was nothing less than to uncover and rethink Being in its proper light.

Husserl took a post at the university of Freiburg, and Heidegger became his protégé, eventually breaking with Husserl's epistemology and method and striking out on his own. The result was *Being and Time*, and the book's success and Husserl's retirement afforded Heidegger the opportunity to take an excellent post at the university. He became its rector in 1933.

He also joined the National Socialist Party. He attended Nazi social gatherings in full socialist regalia. In his inaugural address, 'The Self-Assertion of the German University', Heidegger went on a little about the spiritual mission of the people, the true destiny of Germany and the role of the new rector in guiding the students and staff in the greater glorification of the German people. In a later speech, he told his students that 'the Führer alone is the present and future German reality and its law'. He reported to the authorities what he took to be the inappropriate thinking of several students and faculty members.

Following the war, the Freiburg Denazification Committee found that Heidegger held a prominent position in the Nazi Party and had incited students against some of his colleagues. He was stripped of his teaching post, pensioned off and forbidden to teach until 1951. Heidegger spent some time in an asylum. He was eventually reinstated as Professor Emeritus but never taught in Germany again. Despite the urgings of prominent friends, Herbert Marcuse among them, Heidegger never commented publicly on or apologized for his activities during the war.

The Question of Being

Being and Time is an unusual and original book, dealing as it does with a peculiar question, what Heidegger calls 'the question of being'. It is Heidegger's contention that philosophical and everyday thinking somehow obscures the true nature of what it is for something to exist, and his project is to uncover and rethink being in its proper light. It is his view that the Pre-Socratic philosophers were somehow genuinely in touch with or had the right conception of being, which philosophy has since managed to bury and obscure. His efforts consist in part in recovering this

Heidegger (right, marked with 'X'), at a Nazi party meeting at the University of Freiburg, where he served as rector throughout the Second World War.

ancient conception. The largest part of the problem is conceptual, and this manifests itself in misleading talk about being. The solution involves us in neologisms, which some find unduly obscurantist. Perhaps some charity is required here. If Heidegger is right, and the language we use clouds an honest grasp of his subject matter, what else can he do but coin new words or use old words in unusual ways?

One such word is 'Dasein', translated variously as 'the entity which each of us himself is' or 'being-in-the-world'. The bare term is used so as to beg no questions, presuppose no notion of person or human being beyond whatever it is that we are. Coming to grips with the nature of being, Heidegger seems to suppose, requires a consideration of a certain sort of being, us, for whom the question 'What is being?' is a fundamental or at least a component part of its nature.

Philosophical misconceptions of the nature of human being abound. Thus Heidegger: '... all conventional, objectifying representations of a capsule-like psyche, subject, person, ego or consciousness in psychology and psychopathology must be abandoned in favour of an entirely different understanding. The new view of the basic constitution of the human being may be called Dasein or being-in-the-world.'

Martin Heidegger, pictured in traditional Bavarian dress, after the Second World War. Heidegger's refusal to apologize for his support for Hitler during the Nazi period resulted in his suspension from teaching from 1945 until 1950.

What is a person?

Consider **Descartes**'s conception of a person as consisting in the intimate union of two distinct substances, one mental and the other physical. We take it that the world of objects is a physical world, but then what to do with the part of us that is mental? If a human being is conceived as one part bodily, an object like any other in the world, and one part mental, a thinking thing entirely unlike physical objects, our fundamental place within the world is thus obscured. In particular, our nature as being-in-the-world, things with an intimate concern with the world, is somehow neglected. The Cartesian view disconnects us from physical reality.

A large part of the project thus entails a fleshing out of the fundamental features of Dasein, a re-conceptualization of whatever it is that we are which takes account of our relation to the world. Heidegger identifies three such features: factuality, existentiality and fallenness.

Features of Dasein

Dasein is, in a sense, already here. A part of the human condition, which Heidegger calls our 'factuality', consists in being thrown in the world, abandoned as it were by some past disaster to a life raft, being already a part of the on-going show. It is possible to have the experience of just waking up in the middle of a life, recognizing that one is where one is as a result of some past facts or decisions over which one now has no control. This is the factuality of Dasein, and it consists in the fact that Dasein has a past through which it is somehow constituted in the present.

Dasein, despite being partially determined by the past, also has a feeling of freedom with respect to the future. Dasein is not just constituted by its fixed past but also by its open, possible future, and the responsibility which attends this. This is the existentiality of Dasein, and it pulls in the opposite direction of factuality, not back to the past but forwards into the future.

If the genuine self consists partly in the recognition of both past determinants and future possibilities, the third feature of Dasein, fallenness, identifies the human capacity to ignore both past and future. As a being in the world, Dasein loses itself in the mundane concerns of the present moment. Past and future horizons shrink to a present vanishing point. It is a simple fact of humanity that we neglect large parts of our nature, our past and future, embedding ourselves in the daily grind. We really do measure out our lives with coffee spoons.

It should be clear by now that the nature of being, as revealed by this consideration of the nature of Dasein, is bound up with time. Coming to a recognition of this is part of Heidegger's answer to the question of being. He writes: 'Temporality temporalizes itself fully in each ecstasy, i.e. in the ecstatic unity of the complete temporalizing of temporality there is grounded the wholeness of the structural complex of existentiality, factuality and fallenness, which comprises the unity of the care-structure.'

The concept of 'Dasein' is translated variously as 'the entity which each of us himself is' or 'being-in-the-world'.

Some might not find the language helpful, but the point is that human time in its entirety requires careful consideration if we are to understand the true nature of being. We have to do better than our current preoccupation with the present. In addition to having a past and a present, human time is essentially a time with a limit. The true meaning of Dasein consists partly in the recognition of past determinants and present concerns, but also in being alive to future possibilities. It requires being alive to one inescapable future possibility in particular: being dead. The authentic self brings its many temporal relations into a kind of unity, in light of past, present and a limited future, and acts in the world on this basis.

There is no question of Heidegger's large influence on recent thinking, particularly on the philosophy of Continental Europe. Certainly he had an effect on **Sartre** and the existentialist movement in philosophy, although he was at pains to distance himself from it. The current preoccupation with deconstruction, in particular in the hands of Jacques Derrida and some feminist philosophers, but also as a form of literary criticism, is certainly owed to Heidegger. Marxists and social critics of nearly every sort find in Heidegger grist for various mills. Heidegger wrote a great deal following his suspension from teaching, much of which has still to be published and translated into English. Given this if nothing else, it is likely that Heidegger's true importance in the history of philosophy has not yet been realized.

MAJOR WORKS

Being and Time (1927)
This is Heidegger's most impressive work. It was his first work of any academic significance, and secured him a full professorship at Marburg University. It is a long, highly technical (some might say obscurantist) analysis of human nature and its fundamental connection to time. It introduces the concept of Dasein, 'being-in-itself', and attempts to discover the essence of this being.

Sir Karl Popper

Sir Karl Popper (1902–94) is certainly among the most influential philosophers of science in the twentieth century, as well as an important critic of Marxism, but his reputation is still under consideration.

REASONABLE PEOPLE DISAGREE ABOUT THE REAL IMPORTANCE OF POPPER, about his actual standing in the history of philosophy. Enthusiasts hold well-attended Popper Conferences, identifying him as the Philosopher of the Century. His loudest detractors point to large muddles in his allegedly best work and make sport of some of Popper's incautious claims about the mind and the objectivity of theories, made late in life. Cooler heads withdraw from the debate, maintaining that we are too close in time to Popper's life and leave it to future philosophers to come to conclusions about his standing. We'll join the last group in the following paragraphs.

Popper was raised in Vienna following the First World War, and the times made a formidable impression on him. Although he was the son of a well-to-do lawyer, he witnessed poverty and political upheaval at first-hand. It moved him enough for him to undertake social work. He helped in a clinic for neglected children operated by the Freudian Alfred Adler, and it is clear that some of the events during this part of his life had an influence on his later philosophy. Probably it motivated his thesis topic; certainly it had an effect on his conception of what distinguishes science from other activities like psychoanalysis.

> *Inductive inference moves from a number of particular observations of types of thing, to a general conclusion about things of that type.*

He became a socialist and then a communist. Following the deaths of student and worker protesters at the hands of police, at least some of Popper's communist acquaintances argued that the deaths were a help to the cause. Popper had different views about the value of human life and the ends of political action. The experience led to his rejection of communism and eventual critique of Marxism.

He attended the University of Vienna, earning a PhD with a thesis on the nature of method in psychology, as well as a qualification to teach mathematics and physics in secondary school. While working as a teacher in schools, his thesis caught the eye of certain members of the Vienna Circle – a group of philosophers, mathematicians, physicists and others who were instrumental in the logical positivist movement in the 1920s and 30s. Popper became a contributor to the Circle's discussions, and members of the group would eventually help Popper publish his first book, *The Logic of Scientific Discovery*. The book was read widely, and Popper was invited to lecture at universities both in the United States and Great Britain.

Popper's parents, both from Jewish families, converted to Lutheranism in the hope of blending into Viennese society and had Popper baptized in the faith. Nevertheless, Popper was regarded as Jewish by the Nazis. His British colleagues had a great deal to do with helping Popper out of Vienna and into a philosophy post at University College, Christchurch, New Zealand. Popper remained there throughout the Second World War, teaching and producing his 'war work': *The Poverty of Historicism* and *The Open Society and Its Enemies*. Following the war, he took a post at the London School of Economics, where he continued to defend his views on the nature of science, politics and epistemology. We'll now consider a part of his philosophy of science.

The Problem of Induction

Since **Hume**, philosophers have been lumbered with the problem of induction. Inductive inferences move from a number of particular observations, where several instances of a type of thing have been observed to possess a certain sort of property, to a general conclusion about all things of that type – whether we have seen them or not. Hence the predictive power associated with induction. This snail eats lettuce; so does this one; and this one; and this one too. So, all snails eat lettuce. I bet the next one I find eats lettuce. Inductive inferences seem supported by a principle of this form: if a very large number of things have been observed under all sorts of different conditions, and every one of them has had a certain kind of property, then all such things have that property. As Hume shows, this principle cannot be justified on either logical or experiential grounds, and those seem to be the only justificatory games in town.

According to the principle of falsifiability, the proposition 'all swans are white' can never be proven; a single instance of a black swan, however, can serve to falsify it.

The worrying fact for the philosophy of science is that science seems to proceed on inductive grounds. It's not just our knowledge of snails, but a very large body of what we take to be paradigmatically justified knowledge, scientific knowledge, knowledge rooted in the rigours of scientific experimentation, which seems jeopardized by the problem of induction. If science depends on induction, and induction has no rational justification, is scientific enquiry therefore irrational? If so, and if you want to find a cure for cancer, why not consult an astrologer instead of a scientist? It's probably cheaper.

We have here the two problems which Popper hopes to solve. In what does the rationality of science consist? What distinguishes science from other enterprises?

Popper attempts to avoid the problem of induction by arguing that scientific rationality consists in the falsification of theories, not the inductive verification of them. The view is based on a neat logical asymmetry. As we've just seen, you can observe as many snails as you like, but still your general theory that all snails eat lettuce will remain unproven. However, if you view just one snail which refuses to eat lettuce, you have produced a disproof of the general theoretical claim. It may be logically impossible to prove the truth of a theory by observation, but just one negative observation is enough to falsify a theory.

Falsifiable Hypotheses

Popper views scientific endeavour as the tentative proposal of hypotheses or conjectures which aim to describe some part of the world or solve some problem, followed by the vigorous attempt to falsify them with experimentation. Not just any general statement or theory counts as a scientific one. Given his views on scientific rationality, Popper argues that science works with falsifiable hypotheses, statements or sets of statements which might be undermined by observation, and this is part of what distinguishes science from other activities.

Some hypotheses are obviously not falsifiable on logical grounds – for example, there's no experimental test which could show that 'Either snails eat lettuce or they don't' is false. However, other instances of non-scientific hypotheses are a little more subtle. Suppose I tax you with my Freudian view that unconscious fears of a father figure actuate human behaviour. A little exasperated, you demand some empirical evidence. We go to a pub to observe human interactions, and spot a man hesitating to assert himself at the bar. I explain this easily as evidence that my theory is correct: the man is afraid of the barman; he sees him as a father figure and fears him; hence his hesitation. On the other hand, had the man banged his fist on the bar, demanding the barman's attention, my theory could accommodate this just as easily: the man is attempting to overcome his fear of the barman, a father figure, by asserting himself.

The point about Freudian theory is that it is not falsifiable; it has no negative empirical consequences.

The point is that the Freudian theory is not falsifiable; it has no negative empirical consequences. Thus, for Popper, it is no piece of science. On the contrary, good science consists in bold conjectures, which make a difference to how our observations ought to turn out. Thus Popper:

> I can therefore gladly admit that falsificationists like myself much prefer an attempt to solve an interesting problem by a bold conjecture, *even (and especially) if it soon turns out to be false*, to any recital of a sequence of irrelevant truisms … in finding that our conjecture is false we shall have learnt much about the truth and shall have got nearer the truth.

You may rightly begin to smell a rat here. Is the claim really that scientists do or ought to try to undermine theories? It is hard to imagine scientists getting the champagne out on the discovery of an observation which conflicts with their pet theory, particularly if they have families to support and reputations to uphold. A number of objections to Popper deny that he has managed to describe or prescribe science in the right way – perhaps he has failed to take account of the social aspect of the scientific endeavour.

The Aim of Science

Further, science has practical aims; in the spirit of **Bacon**, we hope that science can improve human life, serve as a basis for choosing and believing. But if we can never know whether or not a theory is true, as Popper has it, then how do we know which of our currently not-yet-falsified theories is the best guide for action? Popper's answer is a little unnerving: theories which have survived ruthless testing should guide us. Unless we fall back into induction, though, we have no reason to think this is true.

It gets much worse, particularly when we carry on thinking about actual situations. First of all, scientific theories are not merely sentences about snails but sometimes vast structures supported by a number of auxiliary hypotheses. Testing situations, too, depend on additional theory, not least theory concerning the proper functioning of equipment, the precise nature of the initial conditions for experimentation. If a falsifying result occurs, one can locate the fault anywhere in a huge pile of theoretical claims and assumptions, keeping the kernel of the theory in place no matter what. If you do not get the result you were hoping for, maybe the machines need recalibrating.

Some argue that observation statements themselves are theory-laden. This is to say that all observations depend on some theory, even very low-level theory. Popper admits this, arguing that observation-statements, like theoretical statements, are themselves tentative, accepted by convention, and susceptible to testing too. He writes:

> The empirical basis of objective science has thus nothing 'absolute' about it. Science does not rest upon solid bedrock. The bold structure of its theories rises, as it were above a swamp. It is like a building erected on piles. The piles are driven down from above into the swamp, but not down to any natural or 'given' base.

Does it make sense to think of theories as things which can be falsified, given all of this? Some think it does, and Popper is not without an army of supporters who continue his work.

MAJOR WORKS

The Logic of Scientific Discovery (1935)

Sets out the doctrine of falsificationism, the view that science proceeds not by induction, but by the deductive demonstration of the falsity of scientific theory. The second part of the work deals with theories, testing, probability, quantum theory and the nature of corroboration.

The Open Society and Its Enemies (1945)

This is Popper's major work in the philosophy of social science. It is a work in two volumes; the first volume is aimed at Plato, specifically his idea of 'philosopher-kings' as the ideal rulers. The second volume deals with Karl Marx. It attempts to explain the rise of totalitarianism and says what ought to be done about it.

Conjectures and Refutations (1963)

Carries on the work of both earlier books, expanding on various falsificationist principles and applying them not just to the philosophy of science but to political philosophy as well.

Jean-Paul Sartre

*Jean-Paul Sartre (1905–80) is the philosopher whose work –
certainly in the English-speaking world – came largely to define
the existentialist movement in the twentieth century.*

THE IMAGE OF THE EXISTENTIALIST AS A CAFÉ-DWELLING, CHAIN-SMOKING, beret-wearing,
intellectual type comes largely from Sartre. And the themes he explored in his writings – particularly the primacy of individual existence, human freedom and the lack
of objective values – are precisely those of existentialism.

Sartre was born into a comfortable, middle-class existence. However, his childhood was far from happy. He was brought up in the home of his maternal
grandfather, Karl Schweitzer – a strict and domineering man – his father having
died when he was just one year old. He was an unattractive child, short in stature
and the victim of an eye condition that made it appear as if his gaze were permanently askance. He had few childhood friends, and spent most of his early life
reading and writing in his grandfather's library. There was also a strange dynamic
between Sartre and his mother; until his grandfather eventually put an end to it, she
pampered him, dressed him in ornate clothing and let his hair grow long.

However, whatever his childhood difficulties, it was clear from very early on
that Sartre was extremely smart. Or as he put it, he was a child prodigy (though
apparently not able to spell too well). Of course, we now know that the prodigy
grew up to be one of the most celebrated intellectuals of the twentieth century.
Sartre is perhaps unique in the breadth of his accomplishments. As well as being a
considerable philosopher, he was also a top-flight novelist, playwright and biogra-
pher. Indeed, in 1964 he was offered the Nobel Prize for Literature, which he
declined saying that he didn't want to be 'transformed into an institution'.

Being and Nothingness

In the case of Sartre, there is something paradoxical in wondering whether his childhood explains the kind of life he lived as an adult, because Sartre is the consummate
philosopher of freedom. He did not think, at least not in any uncomplicated way,
that people are condemned to live certain kinds of lives by the events which occur
in their past. Indeed, it is a common view about Sartre that he is a kind of radical
humanist, concerned with the requirement which individuals face to choose their
own lives and the morals that they espouse. However, although there is something
right about this view, the truth about Sartre's philosophy is more strange than might
at first be supposed.

Some of this strangeness derives from the way that he conceptualized consciousness and the human subject. In *Being and Nothingness* (1943), his major existential work, Sartre divided being into two primary realms: being for-itself, which is consciousness; and being in-itself, which is everything else. He argued that the for-itself is characterized by *nothingness* – that is, emptiness lies right at the heart of being. What did he mean by this? In simple terms, he meant that there is no human essence. Consciousness is permanently detached from the given order of things. It is pure, empty possibility, and therein lies its freedom.

This is a complicated idea. Some light can be shed on it by considering Sartre's treatment of the concept of *negation*. This concerns the capacity to conceive of what is not the case. It is manifest in a whole series of attitudes that the for-itself can adopt towards the objects to which it is directed. Perhaps most significant is the ability of the for-itself to project beyond the given present to an open future of unrealized possibilities – to imagine what *might* be the case. In this sense, the freedom of the for-itself is the permanent possibility that things might be other than they are. Human beings do not find this freedom easy to live with. With the realization that the future is always radically in doubt comes *anguish*. Sartre argued that

To identify oneself in the role of 'waiter', Sartre maintains, is an example of bad faith; a subsumation of one's absolute freedom within an adopted role.

in order to escape anguish individuals adopt strategies of *bad faith*, that is, they seek to deny the freedom that is inevitably theirs.

Bad Faith

There are a couple of very famous examples which illustrate this point. Sartre asked us to imagine a liaison between a woman and a man who she knows wants to seduce her. He takes her hand, but rather than facing up to the requirement to accept or reject him, the woman pretends not to notice; she leaves her hand there as if she were just a passive object. In this way, by, as it were, denying her own subjectivity, she avoids the obligation to choose. The second example involves an over-zealous café waiter who plays his role with just a bit too much care. Sartre's idea here is that the waiter is attempting to subsume himself within his role; to make it as if everything he says and does is determined by his 'waiterhood'. Of course, for Sartre the reality is quite different. The man chose to be a waiter, and at every instance he makes the choice again, because no person has the kind of identity that the waiter seeks in his waiterhood.

A kind of bad faith can also enter into the way that people think about matters of morality. For example, individuals can attempt to flee the freedom which is theirs by adopting an attitude of *seriousness* towards a perceived moral sphere. That is, they might portray their actions as entirely governed by a binding moral code: 'I'd like to help you, but I *can't*, it would be wrong.' Of course, as far as Sartre is concerned, this is just so much rationalization. In his popular *Existentialism and Humanism*, he considers the case of a young man who is confused about whether or not to join the French Free Forces to fight the Germans or whether to stay at home to look after his mother. He shows that it is very difficult to see that there are any clear guides to action in such a situation. Christian ethics, for example, does-

MAJOR WORKS

The Transcendence of the Ego (1936)

This work develops a phenomenological account of the ego, which is specified as a construct rather than the indivisible source of a person's behaviour and character.

La Nausee (1938)

Perhaps Sartre's major existentialist novel, in which he explores the philosophical implications of the contingency of existence through the experiences, charted in a diary, of its main character, Antoine Roquentin.

Sketch for a Theory of Emotions (1939)

In contrast to the traditional view, which sees emotions as largely unchosen, this work articulates the view that they are actively constructed in order to transform our experience of the world.

Being and Nothingness (1943)

Sartre's major work is primarily given over to an analysis of being-for-itself (or consciousness). It features groundbreaking discussion of anguish, bad faith, the spirit of seriousness, being-for-others, and other central elements of existentialism.

Existentialism and Humanism (1948)

Popular work in which Sartre defends existentialism against some of the criticisms which had been levelled against it. Features discussions of 'abandonment' and the absence of an objective moral sphere.

Critique of Dialectical Reason (1960)

A Marxist makeover of existentialism. It represents a retreat from the existentialist emphasis on radical freedom, stressing instead the historical and social constraints on human choice.

n't offer any way of deciding between the general aim of fighting for the whole community and the precise aim of helping one particular person to live. Sartre concludes that all that it is possible to say is that the moral choices that individuals make are theirs and theirs alone, and they are fully responsible for them. All people can do is to choose authentically in the full recognition that they choose freely.

However, the fact that the for-itself is always and inevitably free does not mean that individuals make their choices in a vacuum. Rather, they face up to the specifics of the situations that they confront – for example, that the thief is carrying a knife – and the facticity of their particular lives. *Facticity* here refers to all the things about an individual that cannot be changed at any given point in time – for example, their age, sex and genetic dispositions. Choices then are made against a particular background, so freedom of consciousness does not translate into the idea that people are free to do absolutely anything at the drop of a hat.

Human Freedom and the Self

Interesting in this regard is the role of the self and its relation to human freedom (the self was first properly discussed in an early work, *The Transcendence of the Ego*). Sartre denied that individuals have essential selves. Indeed, part of what defines his philosophy as existentialist is his claim that existence precedes essence. We exist first; the self that we subsequently become is a construct that is built and rebuilt out of experiences and behaviour. In principle, then, the self is something which can be changed, it can be reconstructed. However, in practice, it is not easy to choose a course of action that is out of character with the *fundamental project* of the self. Consequently, the self that we have become imposes another limit on the practice of the freedom that belongs inevitably to the for-itself.

In this treatment of Sartre's ideas, we have concentrated on the philosophical foundations of his idea of freedom. As a result, his philosophy comes out looking as though it is almost entirely concerned with the individual. This is something of a distortion. It would have been possible to have entered Sartre's work at a different point – for example, with his later book, *Critique of Dialectical Reason* – and to have painted a different kind of picture. His commitment to Leftist politics, his interest in the dynamics of social groups, and the fact that he lived at a time of massive political and social upheaval meant that he was almost bound to move beyond the concerns of his early work. Indeed, by the 1960s, with the popularity of structuralism and the emergence of post-structuralism and post-modernism in continental Europe, Sartre's earlier existentialist philosophy had largely fallen into disrepute.

Fashion in intellectual circles is never constant, and there has been something of a revival of interest in Sartre's work.

However, fashion in intellectual circles is never constant, and there has been something of a revival of interest in Sartre's work. Certainly, Sartre remained close to the heart of the French people right up until his death in 1980. His funeral in Paris was attended by more than 20,000 people, and the crowds were so dense that his long-term partner Simone de Beauvoir was almost mobbed as she arrived at the cemetery. Twenty-five years later, people are still visiting his grave, now shared with de Beauvoir, to pay their respects.

A.J. Ayer

Alfred Jules Ayer (1910–1989) was an empiricist philosopher in the British tradition of Locke, Berkeley and Hume, and did much to popularize logical positivism in the English-speaking world.

THERE'S AN AWFUL LOT OF UNIVERSE OUT THERE TO THINK ABOUT – pick a snail no one's noticed and you're off. It is not so easy to be an original philosopher. We've had nearly 2,500 years of thinking, undertaken by the brightest people imaginable, on about four questions. Good luck to anyone who dreams of effecting a philosophical paradigm shift. So it's a little hard to take seriously the hiccoughs which accompany many treatments of A.J. Ayer's philosophy. It is said that he was a brilliant but unoriginal thinker; he brought the views of others to the English-speaking world; he was a great synthesizer of the thoughts of others. You can be all of these things and still be one of the twentieth-century's greatest philosophers. If nothing else, he carried the tradition of British empiricism, a noble line stretching back to **Locke**, **Berkeley** and **Hume**, into the contemporary era. Perhaps this approach to Ayer's philosophy is a cure for the hiccoughs. It's the one adopted here.

Ayer was born in London to Jules Ayer, who came to England from Switzerland when he was 17, and Reine Citroen, her uncle lending the family name to the car company he established. An only child, his early youth was a little lonely, modestly brightened by attending Eton and eventually enlivened at Christ Church College at Oxford. There, he read history and philosophy and, at the suggestion of his tutor, the formidable Gilbert Ryle, he spent an academic year in Vienna, attending meetings of the Vienna Circle. The year's study resulted in *Language, Truth and Logic*, which, despite its brevity, was one of the last century's largest books.

Ayer distinguishes between two sorts of genuine proposition: relations of ideas, and matters of fact.

His research lectureship at Oxford was interrupted when he was called up in 1940 and joined the Welsh Guards, eventually doing intelligence work, including the interrogation of German prisoners. He and his first wife separated during the war. His private life for some time consisted in casual relationships and, eventually, two more marriages. His relationships were more than a little complicated.

Following the war, he was made Grote Professor at University College London, where he transformed the department into a fierce, vigorous centre of philosophical activity. By all accounts he was suited to London life, particularly London's nightlife. Following 13 years at University College, Ayer was elected, with fleeting controversy, to the Wykeham Chair at Oxford, where he continued until 1979. He remained active after his retirement, philosophically, politically, and socially.

Much is made of his near-death experience, probably too much, which occurred when his heart stopped for several minutes before he was finally revived. It had something to do with a bright red light which governed the universe, ministers in charge of space and time, and possibly the River Styx. It is not clear if Ayer himself made much of it. A humanist and free-thinker throughout his life, he called himself a 'born again atheist' after the experience.

Language, Truth and Logic, published when he was 24, is by Ayer's admission 'a young man's book ... written with more passion than most philosophers allow themselves to show'. The book is gutsy, and this is a large part of its attraction. He claims to have dispensed with metaphysics, characterized the nature of meaning and truth, reduced the claims of ethics to expressions of emotion, proved theism nonsensical, solved the problem of induction, dealt with the problems of self and the external world, and provided a conception of the true aim and purpose of philosophy. Not bad for a little more than 150 crisp pages.

Facts and Ideas

The book's core is constituted by a principle which determines whether or not a proposition is meaningful or significant; the conclusions of the book derive from it. Following Hume and the logical positivists of the Vienna Circle, Ayer distinguishes between two sorts of genuine proposition. In Hume's terminology, the distinction is between relations of ideas and matters of fact. The former are the necessary propositions of maths and logic, and the latter are empirical propositions, propositions which depend for their truth or falsity on the way the world actually is. There are other propositions too – propositions not true or false in virtue of symbolic convention or the actual nature of the world. As we shall see, Ayer, like Hume, regards these as pseudo-propositions. However, Ayer goes further, giving an account of just what it is which makes some propositions meaningful and others meaningless.

Tautologies and the statements of mathematics and logic are interesting in their own right, but the philosophical action here is clearly concerned with distinguishing between empirical as against pseudo-propositions. Ayer argues that the verification principle should guide us. He writes:

> The criterion which we use to test the genuineness of apparent statements of fact is the criterion of verifiability. We say that a sentence is factually significant to any given person, if, and only if, he knows how to verify the proposition which it purports to express – that is, if he knows what observations would lead him, under certain conditions, to accept the proposition as being true or reject it as being false.

The principle is not without provisos. Ayer distinguishes between practical verifiability and verification in principle. 'The far side of the moon is mountainous' might not have been practically verifiable when Ayer went to Eton, but it was verifiable in principle. The observations required for determining the truth or falsity of the claim were known, but it was a practical impossibility to carry them out. Still, Ayer argues, the sentence has significance, given the possibility of verification in principle.

A.J. Ayer

Ayer makes another distinction between weak and strong verifiability. According to the strong version, espoused by the Vienna Circle, only conclusive verifiability will do. According to the weak version adopted by Ayer, merely the possibility of observations which render a statement probable is required. Ayer plumps for weak verifiability to get around certain difficulties attending propositions about the past and general theoretical statements. Such claims might never be conclusively verified, but observation can make a difference to thinking them probably true or false, and this is enough to distinguish them from meaningless propositions, according to Ayer.

The fallout for transcendent metaphysics is substantial. What possible sense experience could verify any claim about the allegedly true or underlying nature of things, things as they are apart from experience? On form, Ayer bristles:

> For we shall maintain that no statement which refers to a 'reality' transcending the limits of all possible sense experience can possibly have any literal significance; from which it must follow that the labours of those who have striven to describe such a reality have all been devoted to the production of nonsense.

The problem is not that the arguments of metaphysicians are shoddy, though they might be, but that their claims are unverifiable and therefore without meaning. In so far as theistic claims are themselves metaphysical in this sense, they too are without literal significance. You would be hard pressed to find an observation which might help one way or the other in determining the probability of the truth of the claim that 'Jesus is your personal saviour'.

Ayer takes a fractionally softer line with respect to statements of value, normative ethical and aesthetic claims. 'Stealing money is wrong', for example, has no empirical consequences and therefore cannot be either true or false. Ayer contends that such expressions merely convey the feelings of the speaker. Thus, if I say 'Stealing money is wrong', 'It is as if I had written "Stealing money !!!" – where the shape and thickness of the exclamation marks show, by a suitable convention, that a special sort of moral disapproval is the feeling which is being expressed.'

MAJOR WORKS

Language, Truth and Logic (1936)
Certainly brought Ayer fame and outlined his interpretation of the verification principle. He puts it to good use, as it gives him a position on metaphysics, truth, ethics, religion, the self and the purpose of philosophy.

The Foundations of Empirical Knowledge (1940)
Gives an account of Ayer's early view, much modified later, that talk of physical objects can be translated into talk of actual and possible sense-contents.

The Problem of Knowledge (1956)
Contains excellent reflection on the problem of induction, as well as an analysis of knowledge partly in terms of a subject's right to be sure of some proposition.

The Central Questions of Philosophy (1973)
Is an excellent book for both the beginner and the advanced student, containing as it does not just introductions to philosophical problems but argumentation for Ayer's own views.

Some object that this version of the emotive theory of ethical discourse – the so-called 'Boo! Hurrah!' theory – misses out something fundamental to morality, particularly what goes on when someone thinks through a moral dilemma or when two people have a disagreement about moral claims. With respect to the latter at least, Ayer argues that moral debate can only really consist in factual disagreements, with argument designed to bring a disputant round to a particular emotional response to the facts.

There are other objections to all of this as well, and the strongest take issue in one way or another with the verification principle itself. What, exactly, 'verifiable' means is a complicated question which Ayer takes pains to address. In the end, though, he writes: 'I have to acknowledge that my answer is not very satisfactory.' Despite the confession, we are still owed a clear conception of a notion which does such heavy lifting for Ayer. Some have also argued that the verification principle, if adopted, shows that the principle itself is meaningless. Ayer's response, that he is offering a definition or analysis of meaning, can be matched by formulating a different definition which keeps metaphysics, religion and the rest.

Language, Truth and Logic was certainly not the end of the road for Ayer. He published a number of important books, most but not all tied to the problems first examined in his early twenties. *The Foundations of Empirical Knowledge* argues that sense-data, the immediate data of outer and inner perception, is the infallibly known basis for knowledge of the empirical world. *The Problem of Knowledge* characterizes knowledge along nearly Platonic lines: a subject knows some proposition if that proposition is true; the subject is sure of it; and the subject has a right to be sure of it. The book is one of the best for those who want a handle on philosophical scepticism and the possible solutions to it. In addition to the many books, it is almost impossible to open a collection of essays in metaphysics and epistemology without bumping into Ayer's writings. He is usually found at the beginning of the collection, as a jumping off point for reflection on current problems. We need Ayer's clarity from the start to understand much of contemporary philosophy.

Panelists for the discussion program The Brains Trust *on BBC Television, including Ayer, poet Stevie Smith and programme chairman, writer Robert Kee.*

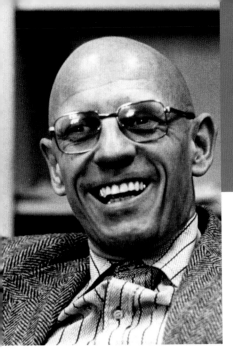

Michel Foucault

Michel Foucault's (1926–84) influence extends beyond philosophy across the humanities and social science. He is perhaps best known for his critiques of various social institutions, most notably psychiatry, medicine and the prison system.

THE BRITISH PHILOSOPHER TED HONDERICH ONCE SAID of late twentieth-century French philosophy 'that it aspires to the condition of literature or the condition of art'; that one thinks of it as 'picking up an idea and running with it, possibly into a nearby brick wall or over a local cliff, or something like that'. It is very easy to find examples of the kind of thing that Honderich is talking about. Here's Jacques Derrida defining the word 'sign' in *Of Grammatology*: '… the sign ~~is~~ that ill-named ~~thing~~, the only one, that escapes the instituting question of philosophy: "what is …?"'

Yes, the crossings out are deliberate. The idea is that the erased words are inadequate to express their intended meaning, but that there aren't any better words either. So they are put 'under erasure'. David Lehman, in his book about deconstruction, *Signs of the Times*, says of this technique that it very quickly becomes an annoying affectation. Many people will agree with him.

Happily, not all modern French philosophy is quite so esoteric. The work of Michel Foucault is a case in point. It is true that in comparison with **Paine** and **Mill**, for example, Foucault is a difficult philosopher. However, he is no more difficult to understand than **Kierkegaard**, and he is considerably easier to get to grips with than **Hegel**. His work also has the merit that it has original and interesting things to say about power, knowledge and subjectivity.

Foucault was born on 15 October 1926 in Poitiers, France, the second child of Anne Malapert and Paul Foucault, a prominent local surgeon and professor of anatomy. His father hoped and expected that his son too would choose to become a doctor. However, it seems that Foucault's family were not the formative influence that they might have been. Rather, in an interview, Foucault suggested that his future ambitions were most profoundly affected by his experience of the Second World War; thus, in 1946, he entered the École Normale Supérieure, graduating in 1951 with degrees in philosophy and psychology. He then went abroad for several years – according to some commentators, in order to escape the conservative sexual mores of French culture – taking up teaching jobs in Sweden, Poland and Germany, before returning to France in 1960 to join the philosophy department at the University of Clermont-Ferrand.

This marked the beginning of the period which established Foucault's intellectual reputation. In 1961, he published his first major work, *Madness and*

Civilization; and he followed this up with eight further books written over a 20-year period, which included *The Order of Things, The Archaeology of Knowledge, Discipline and Punish* and *The History of Sexuality*.

Power and the Self

These works show Foucault mapping out a new course for French philosophy in the latter part of the twentieth century. He drew upon the disciplines of philosophy, history, psychology and sociology in an attempt to show how power and knowledge interact to produce the human subject, or, the self. His intention was to demonstrate that human beings are constituted as knowing, knowable and self-knowing subjects in relations of power and discourse, which necessitated rethinking the concept of power, and analysing the links between power and knowledge.

Foucault claims modern western societies are characterized by three modes of objectification which function to constitute human beings as subjects. These modes are: 'dividing practices'; 'scientific classification'; and 'subjectification'.

Dividing practices objectify people by distinguishing and separating them from their fellows on the basis of distinctions, such as normal and abnormal, sane and insane, the permitted and the forbidden. It is by means of dividing practices that people are categorized, for instance, as madmen, prisoners and mental patients. These categories provide human subjects with the identities through which they will recognize themselves and be recognized by others. Thus, in *Madness and Civilization*, Foucault analysed the mechanisms by which madness was established as a specific category of human behaviour, one which legitimized the detention of individuals in institutions.

The mode of scientific classification objectifies by means of the discourses and practices of the human and social sciences. For instance, it is possible to break down mental illness into the numerous categories of the American Psychiatric Association's *Diagnostic and Statistical Manual of Mental Disorders*; in the *Birth of the Clinic*, Foucault showed how the emergence of the human sciences in the 19th century led to the human body being treated as an 'object' to be analysed, labelled and cured, something which is still characteristic of modern medicine today.

Subjectification is slightly different from the first two modes of objectification in that it refers to the way in which people actively constitute *themselves* as subjects. This idea runs through Foucault's *History of Sexuality*, where he analyses how the desire to understand oneself leads to our confessing our most personal thoughts, feelings and desires both to ourselves and to others. This necessarily implicates us in networks of power relations with authority figures – for example, doctors, psychiatrists and, in the 21st century, perhaps even TV producers – who maintain that they can understand our confessions and reveal the truth of them. It was Foucault's contention that through the expansion of this process of confession, people become objects of their own knowledge and of other people's knowledge; objects, moreover, who have learned how to reconstitute and change themselves. He argued that this phenomenon is a central part of the expansion of the technologies for the control and discipline of bodies and populations in modern societies.

The general process of the objectification of the human subject is linked to historical changes in the nature of power, and to corresponding developments in the areas of human and scientific knowledge. Foucault used the expression 'power/knowledge' to denote this conjunction of power and knowledge. Instead of focusing on coercion, repression and prohibition, he showed how power *produces* human subjects and the knowledge that we have of them. This idea has its fullest expression in the notion of 'bio-power'.

Foucault noted that in the course of the seventeenth century, state power began to make its presence felt in all parts of a person's life; then, with the emergence of industrial capitalism, there was a move away from the use of physical force as a kind of negative power towards new, more effective, technologies of power, which were productive and aimed to foster human life. The state started to focus on the growth and health of its population. Foucault argued that a new regime of bio-power had become dominant, which aimed at the management and administration of the human species or population, and the control or 'discipline' of the human body.

State Power and State Control

In *Discipline and Punish* (1975), Foucault showed how Jeremy Bentham's idea of the panopticon, a type of prison, was a paradigmatic example of disciplinary technology. The panopticon is built in such a way that it functions effectively whether or not prison guards are actually present. Prisoners have no way of knowing whether they are being watched, and so they must behave as if surveillance were constant and never ending. Effectively, then, prisoners become their own guardians. Thus, according to Foucault, the panopticon brings together power, knowledge, the control of the body and the control of space into a single, integrated disciplinary technology. The parallels here with wider society are clear. Society exerts its greatest power to the extent that it produces individual human subjects

MAJOR WORKS

Madness and Civilisation (1961)

An analysis of the genesis of modern psychology, it attacks the idea that 'madness' and 'mental illness' are natural categories, suggesting instead that they exist at the intersection of various institutional, social and political imperatives.

Birth of the Clinic (1963)

This work, the first of Foucault's archaeological studies, shows how the emergence of the human sciences, and medical science, in particular, led to the human body being treated as an 'object' to be analysed, labelled and cured.

The Order of Things (1966)

A complex analysis of the 'epistemes' – the systems of thought and knowledge – which, across time, have underpinned various kinds of social scientific enquiry. It pursues the claim that different ages have a different understanding of the relations between language and truth.

The Archaeology of Knowledge (1969)

A theoretical articulation of the archaeological method which had underpinned his previous historical studies. A difficult book, it introduces the new concept of a discursive formation, which 'presents the principle of articulation between a series of discursive events and other series of events, transformations, mutations, and processes'.

Discipline and Punish (1975)

A study of the emergence of the modern prison, and, more generally, a disciplinary technology which functions to classify and control human subjects.

The History of Sexuality (3 volumes, 1976, 1984, 1984)

These three volumes represent the beginnings of a study on human sexuality which Foucault never completed. The most mature expression of Foucault's thoughts about biopower and biopolitics.

who police themselves in terms of the discourses and practices of sexual, moral, physical and psychological normality.

Foucault's concern with matters to do with power and the control of populations and bodies was mirrored in his political activities; he was, throughout his adult life, interested in issues to do with gay rights, prison reform, mental health and the welfare of refugees. However, there is something slightly paradoxical in this, for it is one of the criticisms of Foucault's work that it functions to undermine any commitment to emancipatory politics. Put simply, the thought here is that by elevating power to the point where it infects everything, Foucault's position rules out the possibility of any genuinely benevolent, or even rational, impulse or intervention. For example, if scientific psychiatry has transformed the lives of 'schizophrenics' through the use of antipsychotic drugs, it is only because it is aimed towards the control of patients, not because it seeks good outcomes for them. Or, to take slightly different example, if truth about history is a function of power, then whether or not the Holocaust took place is not a matter of historical fact, but rather a matter of establishing, or not establishing, the dominance of particular historical narratives.

Many of Foucault's critics claim that his views lead straight to a relativism about both truth and morals. For example, Patrick West argued in the *New Statesman*:

> The pervading theme in Foucault's philosophy is that human relations are defined by the struggle for power. Right and wrong, truth and falsehood, are illusions. They are the creation of language and the will to dominate … Thus, there is no such thing as benevolence: men have created hospitals, schools and prisons not to cure, educate and reform, but to control and dominate 'the Other'. The rationalism of the Enlightenment was merely a mask for this malevolent impulse.

There is certainly something right about this criticism. Indeed, the influence of thinkers like Foucault has been declining in recent years precisely because it has been recognized that their nihilist leanings undermine the possibility of genuine political commitment. Nevertheless, even if one wishes to reject the more radical aspects of Foucault's approach, it would be wrong to dismiss his work in its entirety. Foucault's importance is that he showed how power *can* operate; that is, to create human bodies, human subjects and populations which in various ways are surveyed, categorized, disciplined and controlled.

Foucault lived his life as if he were driven by the need to transcend both physical and cultural limits. He experimented with LSD, visited sadomasochistic clubs in California, attempted more than once to kill himself, and talked of the intense pleasure he had experienced after being hit by a car. In the end, he was killed by an AIDS-related illness; he was one of the first victims of a disease he presumably thought only properly existed in the context of particular discourses or narratives.

Writing desk in the home of Michel Foucault.

Index

The references to people in bold, as Aristotle **16-19,** refer to the main entries for those individuals

Picture Credits